THE LOST
- AND FOUND -
JOURNAL OF

X_____

A YEAR IN THE LIFE OF THE
AWESOMEST GIRL WHO EVER LIVED

JANUARY-JUNE

J.C. DUBLIN

Trade Paperback Edition ISBN: 978-1-7339429-6-6

Cover illustration by Tithi Luadthong

Printed in these United States of America

OLDENWORLD BOOKS

www.JackDublin.net

To movers and shakers and history makers

HOW TO USE YOUR JOURNAL

This isn't rocket science. It's not even bicycle science. But it just might be journaling science, which can take you faster, farther, and higher than bikes or rockets if you agree to one principle: *nothing is impossible.*

In the pages stacked at your right hand, you will encounter inventors, conquerors, saints, and scoundrels who left their mark on the world in their own way. We may think Alexander the Great and Orville Wright were nothing alike—nor Emma Snodgrass (arrested numerous times for wearing pants) and Louis Lassen (inventor of the hamburger), for that matter—but they all shared something in common. They all burned within from ideas they wouldn't let die.

Most of you... no, I take that back... ALL of you reading this have ideas smoldering within that yearn for a sufficient gust of air to spark them into flames. When that happens... look out! I'll need to update this journal to account for the day you achieved your dreams.

This journal is very simple to use. On the next two pages you will find samples of a Daily Page (e.g. July 31) and what I call the monthly *Outro* Page.

The Daily Page examines an historical event from that day in history and provides you with a **writing** prompt and an **action** prompt.

The *Outro* Page falls at the end of each month and is a place to record remarkable events that happened to you over the month. It also serves to set your sights on achieving your goals. Talk is cheap… action is priceless. So, get busy!

Finally, at the end of this book you will find three pages dedicated to writing about your 6-month goals, 3-year goals, and lifetime goals. If you're not writing down your goals, you're unlikely to go anywhere interesting in life.

So, the choice is yours: dutifully write in this journal every day and become the best possible version of you, or approach the task with yawns and bitter protests and become something less than that. I promise I will never show up at your door to twist your arm. The path you choose is entirely up to you.

Best success,
J.C.

On this day in 1703: Author is placed in pillory in Lond⟨...⟩

⟨...⟩ism of the⟨...⟩

Dive In: The pillory boards. Onlookers a⟨...⟩ with rotten eggs a⟨...⟩

Speak Up: Peopl⟨...⟩ the cold hard tr⟨...⟩

The event might've happened last year or 1,000's of years ago, but it's sure to get you thinking!

Find out more about the event here. It's in the details that the truth may seem stranger than fiction!

Now it's your turn to speak up! What's on your mind? What can you learn from this historical event?

"Sample Daily Page"

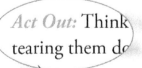

Act Out: Think tearing them d⟨...⟩

Talking is for talkers... doing is for doers. Turn your thoughts into action!

"Sample Outro Page"

Time Capsule: ___

This is the stuff you will tell your kids and grandkids when you get old. Could be a world event, a personal victory, or a funny joke you heard.

I chased my dreams by: ___

Waking dreams (goals) are like sleeping dreams (illusions)... both fade in time if you don't talk about them or write them down. Don't let go of yours!

I made the world a better place by: ___

You might not save the world, but you can leave a lasting glow in someone's life with a kind deed, a timely compliment, or even a simple smile.

I'm looking forward to: ___

Everyone needs stuff to look forward to. What's on your calendar? Might be a vacation, a sleepover with friends, or competing in an event.

Next play: ___

If you achieved a goal this month, great job! But don't sit around patting yourself on the back. What dragon do do you want to slay next?

JANUARY
INTRO

"You may find the worst enemy or best friend in yourself."

– English Proverb

JANUARY 1

On this day in 2019: The New Horizons spacecraft makes history with the flyby of Ultima Thule, a mysterious object 4.1 billion miles from Earth in the Kuiper Belt, a frigid outer region of the solar system.

Dive In: The event marked the farthest flyby of an object in our solar system. Pictures revealed Ultima Thule kind of looks like a red snowman!

Speak Up: If you could go somewhere no one has gone before, where would it be?

_____

_____

_____

_____

_____

_____

_____

_____

_____

_____

_____

_____

_____

_____

Act Out: Go somewhere today you've never gone before!

JANUARY 2

On this day in 1906: Willis Carrier receives a US patent for the world's first modern air conditioning system.

Dive In: Early January is a strange time to be thinking about air conditioners, but the invention allowed millions of people to live comfortably in areas they might not otherwise have chosen to live, such as Phoenix, AZ (the fifth most populous city in the US).

Speak Up: If you had to live in the desert, what would be the one thing you would have to have (other than air conditioning)?

_____

_____

_____

_____

_____

_____

_____

_____

_____

_____

_____

_____

_____

Act Out: If it's winter where you live, step outside of your warm house and into the cold air. Appreciate that people mastered temperature controls for your comfort.

JANUARY 3

On this day in 1496: Leonardo da Vinci unsuccessfully tests a flying machine made of pinewood and silk.

Dive In: Ouch! It sounds like Leonardo may have suffered some bumps and bruises. But that's the price of discovery. In order to achieve your wildest dreams, you will endure lumps along the way.

Speak Up: Are there any "bumps or bruises" you wouldn't suffer to achieve your dream?

_____
_____
_____
_____
_____
_____
_____
_____
_____
_____
_____
_____
_____
_____
_____
_____

Act Out: Design a paper airplane and see how far it flies.

JANUARY 4

On this day in 1959: Luna 1 becomes first craft to leave Earth's gravity. The Russians call it "Artificial Planet 1".

Dive In: Ah, escape from Earth's gravity! The idea has stewed in the minds of men since Isaac Newton first identified the force of gravity while his school was shuttered because of the Black Plague pandemic of 1666. Many of you readers may be home from school because of a pandemic shutdown right now.

Speak Up: What world-changing discovery would you like to make during a shutdown of your school?

_____

_____

_____

_____

_____

_____

_____

_____

_____

_____

_____

_____

_____

_____

_____

Act Out: Go learn one other interesting fact about Isaac Newton that you don't already know.

JANUARY 5

On this day in 1834: Kiowa Indians witness an event they record as "the night the stars fell."

Dive In: On the wintery American plains nearly two hundred years ago, the light of so many shooting stars in the night sky awoke the Kiowa Indians who believed morning had come. When they saw the source of light was not the sun, but blazing meteors, they believed the end of the world was upon them.

Speak Up: If you ever witnessed an event like that, would you be afraid, or joyously make as many wishes as you could?

_____

_____

_____

_____

_____

_____

_____

_____

_____

_____

_____

_____

_____

_____

Act Out: If the sky is clear tonight, see if you can spot a shooting star.

JANUARY 6

On this day in 1838: Samuel Morse first demonstrates the telegraph device in Morristown, NJ, USA.

Dive In: In an age of cell phones, tablets, texting and Zoom, a machine that can only communicate with beeps doesn't sound like a big deal, but in those days it was the fastest way to communicate at a distance.

Speak Up: What's your favorite way to communicate with people who are far away?

_____

_____

_____

_____

_____

_____

_____

_____

_____

_____

_____

_____

_____

_____

_____

_____

Act Out: Build a "telephone" with a pair of empty cans connected by a string. Can you hear the person on the other end of the line?

JANUARY 7

On this day in 1610: Galileo Galilei discovers the first three moons of Jupiter: Io, Europa, and Ganymede. These, along with Callisto, are known as the Galilean moons.

Dive In: While quite a feat for Galileo's time, in our age anyone with a decent pair of binoculars can see these three moons, plus a fourth!

Speak Up: If you discovered a new world, what would you name it and why?

_____

_____

_____

_____

_____

_____

_____

_____

_____

_____

_____

_____

_____

_____

_____

_____

Act Out: Grab a pair of binoculars and go find Jupiter. Can you see the four brightest moons around it?

JANUARY 8

On this day in 1877: Crazy Horse and his warriors fight their final battle with the US Cavalry at the Battle of Wolf Mountain (near modern day Birney, MT, USA).

Dive In: Long after the Lakota leader's death, he was remembered for his heroics in battle, so much so that a memorial to him is being carved in the Black Hills of South Dakota. The monument, when complete, will be larger than Mount Rushmore!

Speak Up: If you could choose any way to be immortalized, how would it be?

_____

_____

_____

_____

_____

_____

_____

_____

_____

_____

_____

_____

_____

_____

_____

_____

Act Out: Find out how many miles you live from the Crazy Horse Memorial.

JANUARY 9

On this day in 2007: Apple CEO Steve Jobs announces the first iPhone with the slogan, "This is only the beginning."

Dive In: Believe it or not, a time existed before the iPhone. Today, they are as ubiquitous as automobiles, but it took the imagination of Jobs to bring the touch-screen device to market.

Speak Up: Have you ever been told a crazy idea you had wouldn't work? Did you give up on your idea? Why or why not?

_____

_____

_____

_____

_____

_____

_____

_____

_____

_____

_____

_____

_____

_____

_____

Act Out: Imagine an invention that would make the world a better place, even if you don't know how to make it work.

JANUARY 10

On this day in 49 BC: Julius Caesar defies the Roman Senate and crosses the Rubicon River, famously saying, "The die is cast."

Dive In: Julius Caesar's action initiated a civil war which resulted in his appointment as dictator for life. Today, "crossing the Rubicon" means to pass a point of no return.

Speak Up: Have you ever done something which you were told not to do? Did your decision turn out good or bad?

_____

_____

_____

_____

_____

_____

_____

_____

_____

_____

_____

_____

_____

_____

_____

_____

Act Out: Come up with a clever phrase you would say if you were passing a point of no return.

JANUARY 11

On this day in 1935: Amelia Earhart flies from Honolulu to Oakland, CA, USA.

Dive In: Adventurers come from all walks of life, but the common denominator is an individual's desire to succeed even in the face of danger. Amelia Earhart demonstrated that desire as a pilot.

Speak Up: Flying from Hawaii to California is a long way (over 2,400 miles). Would you be afraid to take a trip that far by yourself? Why or why not?

_____

_____

_____

_____

_____

_____

_____

_____

_____

_____

_____

_____

_____

Act Out: Imagine a journey you might take by yourself to a far and distant land. Would you go by foot, horse, car, plane, spaceship, or some other form of transportation?

JANUARY 12

On this day in 2010: An earthquake destroys most of Port-au-Prince, Haiti, killing approximately 160,000 people.

Dive In: Earthquakes can be scary events, especially when they are strong enough to destroy entire cities.

Speak Up: Do you worry about natural disasters where you live, such as earthquakes, fires, hurricanes, or floods? Why or why not?

_____

_____

_____

_____

_____

_____

_____

_____

_____

_____

_____

_____

_____

_____

_____

_____

_____

_____

Act Out: Prepare a backpack of items that would help you survive if you had to flee your home on a moment's notice.

JANUARY 13

On this day in 1610: Galileo discovers Callisto, the fourth known moon of Jupiter.

Dive In: Wow! Six days ago, we learned that Galileo discovered three worlds on one day in 1610. Then, he discovers a fourth world, increasing the known number of celestial bodies in our solar system by more than 50% in less than a week.

Speak Up: If you could travel to any moon of Jupiter, which one would you visit and why? This requires that you learn something about the moons of Jupiter!

_____

_____

_____

_____

_____

_____

_____

_____

_____

_____

_____

_____

_____

_____

Act Out: Make a list of items you would need to survive one week on the Moon.

JANUARY 14

On this day in 1514: Pope Leo X issues a papal bull (official document) against slavery.

Dive In: Slavery is the awful condition where a person is treated as someone's property. Even so, slavery has been a common condition throughout human history.

Speak Up: When Leo X issued his condemnation of slavery, many opposed his decision. Do you ever lack the courage to say something because you think other people won't agree with you?

_____

_____

_____

_____

_____

_____

_____

_____

_____

_____

_____

_____

_____

Act Out: Think of something you see every day that you wish wasn't so. Now, list three ways you might convince other people to help you stop it from happening.

JANUARY 15

On this day in 588 BC: Nebuchadnezzar II of Babylon attacks Jerusalem during King Zedekiah's reign.

Dive In: For two-and-a-half years, Nebuchadnezzar besieged Jerusalem. While the residents of Jerusalem fought valiantly, they eventually fell to the nation of Babylon.

Speak Up: Do you ever feel like you are in a situation that you can't win? Do you continue to resist, or do you submit?

_____

_____

_____

_____

_____

_____

_____

_____

_____

_____

_____

_____

_____

_____

Act Out: Today, Jerusalem survives as a city, but Babylon is buried in the dust of history. No matter how dark your future looks, take heart in the history of others who battled giants. Now, think of one way that you are weak and afraid and vow to make yourself strong and courageous.

JANUARY 16

The impeachment trial of US President Donald J. Trump begins in the Senate.

Dive In: Impeachment (recommendation to remove an elected representative from office) of a US President has only happened three times in history, with Andrew Johnson, William J. Clinton, and Donald J. Trump. None of the three impeachments succeeded in removing the President.

Speak Up: Even if you knew that impeaching a President would not likely remove him or her from office, would you still vote to impeach if you were convinced that person did something wrong?

_____
_____
_____
_____
_____
_____
_____
_____
_____
_____
_____
_____

Act Out: Someone once said that you should speak the truth even if your voice trembles. Make a vow to yourself to stand up against any injustice you see in the world.

JANUARY 17

On this day in 1733: Captain James Cook becomes the first known explorer to cross the Antarctic Circle.

Dive In: Due to ice and fog, Captain Cook turned back, not realizing he was only 80 miles from discovering Antarctica.

Speak Up: Have you ever given up hope on some project or plan, only to later realize how close you were to succeeding?

_____

_____

_____

_____

_____

_____

_____

_____

_____

_____

_____

_____

_____

_____

_____

_____

_____

Act Out: Resolve that if you have a goal, you will not turn back from realizing it, even if the world tells you to go home!

JANUARY 18

On this day in 1535: Francisco Pizarro founds the city of Lima, Peru.

Dive In: Nearly 500 years later, the city of Lima still stands. Old cities like this always have a starting point, but over time we forget that they weren't always there.

Speak Up: Can you think of something you see every day that you would miss if it wasn't around?

_____

_____

_____

_____

_____

_____

_____

_____

_____

_____

_____

_____

_____

_____

_____

_____

_____

Act Out: Design a monument to the most important thing in your life (could be a drawing, sculpture, song, or poem).

JANUARY 19

On this day in 1883: The first electric lighting system using overhead wires, designed by Thomas Edison, is switched on in Roselle, NJ, USA.

Dive In: In the old days, when the sun went down, you built a fire or lit a candle to have light. Then, gas lighting came along. But lighting by electricity was a game changer because it offered an inexpensive and highly expandable way to light the darkness.

Speak Up: Are you afraid of the dark? Why or why not?

_____

_____

_____

_____

_____

_____

_____

_____

_____

_____

_____

_____

_____

Act Out: If you are afraid of the dark, stand in a dark place and say to yourself, 'I have nothing to fear but fear itself.' (That's a paraphrased saying of US President Franklin Roosevelt.)

JANUARY 20

On this day in 1986: The first national holiday celebrating the life and legacy of Martin Luther King, Jr.

Dive In: Few people in human history made such an impact with so few years as Martin Luther King, Jr. He inspired a nation to not judge others "by the color of their skin but by the content of their character."

Speak Up: Have you ever judged someone based on something they could not control (the way they look, the way they speak, the place they come from)?

_____
_____
_____
_____
_____
_____
_____
_____
_____
_____
_____
_____
_____
_____

Act Out: Stand in front of a mirror. Now, tell yourself you look beautiful, you speak with the voice of an angel, and the places you've been matter less than the place you call home.

JANUARY 21

On this day in 1853: An envelope-folding machine is patented by Russell Hawes in Worcester, MA, USA.

Dive In: Several of this author's close relatives attended college in Worcester, but that's not why I point out this invention to you. Many years ago, the office I worked in suffered from inefficiency and I suggested we buy an envelope-folding machine to help our team. Did it work? Yes! And how thankful everybody was for that machine.

Speak Up: Adversity is a rich minefield for new inventions. Why do you think people strive to make their jobs easier?

_____

_____

_____

_____

_____

_____

_____

_____

_____

_____

_____

_____

Act Out: Think of something you hate to do. Now, write down why you hate it and list three things that would make it easier. You're on your way to inventing something new!

JANUARY 22

On this day in 2020: China locks down Wuhan, a city of 11 million people, after 17 people die from a new strain of coronavirus.

Dive In: You might not think a city of 11 million people would need to be locked down after 17 people died. But in this case the Chinese acted too slowly—within 8 months, worldwide coronavirus related deaths would surpass 800,000.

Speak Up: How would you warn your neighbors about a deadly threat to your neighborhood?

_____
_____
_____
_____
_____
_____
_____
_____
_____
_____
_____
_____
_____

Act Out: Wash your hands with soap and water for twenty seconds to keep them germ-free. How long is twenty seconds? About as long as it takes you to sing the *Happy Birthday* song twice!

JANUARY 23

On this day in 1930: Astronomer Clyde Tombaugh photographs an unknown object in the heavens, leading to the discovery of Pluto.

Dive In: Tombaugh was not the first person to photograph Pluto. Percival Lowell photographed the dwarf planet twice in 1915 but, sadly, he never recognized the faint point of light for what it was.

Speak Up: Have you ever missed out on something big because you didn't think it was valuable at the time?

_____

_____

_____

_____

_____

_____

_____

_____

_____

_____

_____

_____

_____

_____

_____

Act Out: Think about something in your life you take for granted. Now, imagine life without that "ordinary" thing.

JANUARY 24

On this day in 1848: James Marshall discovers gold in a stream at Sutter's Mill in Coloma, CA, USA.

Dive In: The story of James Marshall's gold find is the opposite of Percival Lowell's picture of Pluto. When Marshall saw gold in a stream bed, he knew exactly what it was and its tremendous worth.

Speak Up: California gold was discovered in early 1848, but the Gold Rush didn't begin for almost a full year. Why do you think the Gold Rush took so long to begin?

_____

_____

_____

_____

_____

_____

_____

_____

_____

_____

_____

_____

_____

Act Out: Panning for gold requires nothing more than a pan, sediment, and water. Give the watery sediment several good shakes in the pan. If there's gold, it will sink to the bottom. Give it a shot!

JANUARY 25

On this day in 1840: Charles Wilkes leads American naval expedition to Antarctica, identifying it as the 7th continent.

Dive In: Today Antarctica is covered in a thick sheet of ice and snow, but it wasn't also so. Remains of an ancient rainforest have been discovered in Antarctica!

Speak Up: How different do you think the world was when Antarctica had trees? What animals might have lived where penguins live today?

_____

_____

_____

_____

_____

_____

_____

_____

_____

_____

_____

_____

_____

_____

_____

_____

Act Out: Draw a made-up animal from ancient Antarctica.

JANUARY 26

On this day in 1926: Scottish inventor John Logie Baird for the first time publicly televises images in motion.

Dive In: This sounds exciting until you realize there weren't any TV channels or video streaming options for Mr. Baird. In fact, the moving images he televised weren't even of real people—they were those of ventriloquist dummies.

Speak Up: If you could travel back in time, what modern TV show would you demonstrate for Mr. Baird?

_____

_____

_____

_____

_____

_____

_____

_____

_____

_____

_____

_____

_____

_____

_____

_____

Act Out: TV and video are everywhere today. Try going a whole day without it.

JANUARY 27

On this day in 1967: During a launch rehearsal of the Apollo 1 Command Module, fire engulfs and kills astronauts Gus Grissom, Ed White, and Roger Chaffee.

Dive In: A sad moment in the U.S. space program that could have ended America's race to the Moon. But it didn't. Two-and-a-half years later, Neil Armstrong and Buzz Aldrin would stand on the Moon.

Speak Up: Have you ever failed at something so badly that you just wanted to quit?

_____
_____
_____
_____
_____
_____
_____
_____
_____
_____
_____
_____
_____

Act Out: The next time you fail (we all fail… a lot!) think about the perseverance after Apollo 1 that led to the glory of Apollo 11. When you fall, get back up!

JANUARY 28

On this day in 1986: US Space Shuttle Challenger explodes 73 seconds after liftoff when engaging full throttle, killing all seven astronauts on board.

Dive In: Among the astronauts was teacher Christa McAuliffe, who won a contest to be among the crew. All great adventurers face great risk, and the Challenger crew was no exception.

Speak Up: In your lifetime you may have the opportunity to vacation in space. Would you want to go on a vacation like that? Why or why not?

_____
_____
_____
_____
_____
_____
_____
_____
_____
_____
_____
_____
_____
_____

Act Out: Think up a name for the first spacecraft that will carry astronauts to the planet Mars.

JANUARY 29

On this day in 1595: First performance of William Shakespeare's play *Romeo and Juliet.*

Dive In: *Romeo and Juliet* is one of the classic plays of all time, a love story for the ages in which a boy and girl from feuding families fall in love. The families conspire against the lovers.

Speak Up: Do you ever feel like some people don't want you to succeed? How do you handle those situations?

_____

_____

_____

_____

_____

_____

_____

_____

_____

_____

_____

_____

_____

_____

Act Out: Write a silly poem about how much you love your pet or favorite toy.

JANUARY 30

On this day in 1873: Jules Verne's novel *Around the World in 80 Days* is published in France.

Dive In: In 1873, traveling around the world in 80 days sounded like an impossible feat. Today, astronauts do it in 90 minutes!

Speak Up: If you could venture anywhere in the world, where would you go?

_____
_____
_____
_____
_____
_____
_____
_____
_____
_____
_____
_____
_____
_____
_____
_____

Act Out: Plan a trip around the world in 80 days using no less than five modes of transportation (i.e., car, camel, boat, hang glider, etc.)

JANUARY 31

On this day in 1865: US Congress passes the 13th Amendment, abolishing slavery in the United States.

Dive In: This amendment was a long time coming, set in motion by the US Constitution itself. Unfortunately, it took a civil war that left over 600,000 Americans dead to realize the vision.

Speak Up: The struggle for freedom is as old as mankind. Is there any principle you would be willing to die for?

_____

_____

_____

_____

_____

_____

_____

_____

_____

_____

_____

_____

_____

_____

_____

Act Out: Write a 25-word freedom statement for a group of people, animals, or… robots?

JANUARY
OUTRO

Time Capsule: _____
_____
_____
_____

I chased my dreams by: _____
_____
_____
_____

I made the world a better place by: _____
_____
_____
_____

I'm looking forward to: _____
_____
_____
_____

Next play: _____
_____

FEBRUARY
INTRO

"Faith is taking the first step even when you don't see the whole staircase."

- Martin Luther King, Jr.

FEBRUARY 1

On this day in 1958: Explorer 1, the first US satellite, launches into space.

Dive In: The space race is on! The USSR and the US vied for space supremacy at a time when color TV was only for the extremely wealthy.

Speak Up: In what ways do you seek to show others that you are the best at what you do?

_____

_____

_____

_____

_____

_____

_____

_____

_____

_____

_____

_____

_____

Act Out: Run a footrace against your fastest family member. How hard will you train to win?

FEBRUARY 2

On this day in 1892: Boxer Harry Sharpe defeats Frank Cosby in 77 rounds, the longest bout ever under modern (Queensberry) rules.

Dive In: The five-hour boxing match was hard on everyone, including the referee who collapsed during the fight. Despite the lack of officiating, the boxers slugged on to the end according to sport rules.

Speak Up: An old adage says that your character is who you are when nobody is watching. If you knew nobody was watching, would you break the rules? Why or why not?

_____

_____

_____

_____

_____

_____

_____

_____

_____

_____

_____

Act Out: Rules make for an orderly society. Read the Ten Commandments and think about why they are important.

FEBRUARY 3

On this day in 1863: Author Samuel Clemens, creator of characters Tom Sawyer and Huckleberry Finn, first uses the pen name Mark Twain in a Virginia City, NV newspaper.

Dive In: Samuel Clemens followed his brother, Orion Clemens, west to Nevada after Abraham Lincoln named Orion the Secretary of the Nevada Territory.

Speak Up: Samuel hoped to strike it rich in the gold and silver bonanzas of the 1860's. He failed miserably. He did, however, learn to write to earn a living. What's the number one way you want to earn a living? If that fails, what's your backup plan?

_____

_____

_____

_____

_____

_____

_____

_____

_____

_____

Act Out: Talent is overrated, but practice breeds success. Begin your #1 plan and backup plans today!

FEBRUARY 4

On this day in 1789: The first US electoral college unanimously chooses George Washington as President, the only unanimously elected President in US history.

Dive In: George Washington was such a respected figure that many of his peers believed the young nation would never have survived without his leadership.

Speak Up: Are you a leader or a follower? What traits do you think a good leader needs to succeed?

_____

_____

_____

_____

_____

_____

_____

_____

_____

_____

_____

_____

_____

Act Out: People want action, not words. If you want to be a leader, lead by example.

FEBRUARY 5

On this day in 1869: World's largest alluvial gold nugget, weighing 173 pounds, found in Victoria, Australia.

Dive In: The nugget yielded 2,284 troy ounces, which is worth over $4 million today!

Speak Up: If you found $4 million worth of gold, what charity would you donate to and why?

_____

_____

_____

_____

_____

_____

_____

_____

_____

_____

_____

_____

_____

_____

_____

_____

Act Out: You may not have $4 million dollars, but everyone has something. Donate to a charity or give a gift to someone in need.

FEBRUARY 6

On this day in 2018: Private company SpaceX launches a rocket called the Falcon Heavy for the first time.

Dive In: The launch was only a test, so instead of carrying a payload (like a satellite) into orbit, it carried a Tesla Roadster sports car and a test dummy named Starman.

Speak Up: Rockets carry not only payloads and astronauts into space, but the cremated ashes of people, too! When you die, would you rather have your ashes launched to the Moon or have a traditional burial on Earth? Why?

_____

_____

_____

_____

_____

_____

_____

_____

_____

_____

_____

_____

Act Out: SpaceX will be assisting NASA with the Artemis program, which will land a man and woman on the Moon in 2024. Learn more at **https://www.nasa.gov/specials/artemis/**

FEBRUARY 7

On this day in 1812: An 8.2 magnitude earthquake strikes New Madrid, Missouri.

Dive In: Operators of flatboats afloat during the earthquake reported the Mississippi river suddenly flowed backwards!

Speak Up: Scientists dispute the operators' claims that the river really flowed backwards. They say a water surge only made it *appear* to flow backwards. Have you ever been convinced of a "truth" only to realize it was illusion?

_____

_____

_____

_____

_____

_____

_____

_____

_____

_____

_____

_____

_____

_____

_____

Act Out: Magicians use illusions to fool people. Learn a magic trick to fool your friends and family.

FEBRUARY 8

On this day in 1986: 5'7" basketball player Spud Webb wins the NBA Slam Dunk Contest.

Dive In: Mr. Webb entered the contest at a considerable disadvantage—the average height of an NBA player is around 6'7"!

Speak Up: When hearing about the achievement of Spud Webb, the saying "the sky's the limit" comes to mind. Do you ever feel at a disadvantage among your siblings, friends, or classmates? How do you overcome those disadvantages?

_____

_____

_____

_____

_____

_____

_____

_____

_____

_____

_____

_____

Act Out: Hard work pays off. If you ever told yourself you couldn't achieve a goal because you were disadvantaged, change your mind. Be like Spud!

FEBRUARY 9

On this day in 1825: The US House of Representatives elects John Quincy Adams as President, even though Andrew Jackson received a plurality of popular and electoral votes.

Dive In: In most elections, the US President is chosen by the electoral college. But if no candidate wins a majority of votes, the House of Representatives decides.

Speak Up: Andrew Jackson didn't give up. Four years later, he won a majority vote in the electoral college and replaced Adams as President. Have you ever fallen short of a goal? If so, did you respond by giving up or trying harder the next time around?

_____

_____

_____

_____

_____

_____

_____

_____

_____

_____

_____

_____

Act Out: Learn the difference between a majority and a plurality.

FEBRUARY 10

On this day in 1990: Under the looming threat of civil war, South African President F.W. de Klerk announces political prisoner Nelson Mandela will be freed the following day.

Dive In: Nelson Mandela spent 27 years in prison for plotting to overthrow the government. After his release, Mandela won the Nobel Peace Prize for ending apartheid (segregation) in South Africa and later became President of his country.

Speak Up: Mandela outlasted the apartheid system he spent his life fighting against. If you were imprisoned, how would you keep hope alive in your heart?

_____

_____

_____

_____

_____

_____

_____

_____

_____

Act Out: Talking to yourself is a proven way to bring change to your life. But be careful—repeating positive words brings good change; repeating negative words brings bad change.

FEBRUARY 11

On this day in 1731: George Washington, the first President of the US, is born (sort of).

Dive In: In Washington's family Bible, his birthday is listed twice: first as February 11, 1731, then as February 22, 1732. So, which was it? The answer, strangely enough, is both. At the time he was born, the British Empire used the Julian calendar (Old Style) to reckon time, but it lagged the Gregorian calendar (New Style) by 11 days. Complicating matters, in the Old Style the British began the New Year on March 25th, but on January 1st under the New Style.

Speak Up: Geesh! Who thought celebrating a birthday could be so difficult? If you were George, what day would you celebrate your birthday? Why?

_____

_____

_____

_____

_____

_____

_____

_____

_____

_____

Act Out: Find out if any world leaders or otherwise famous people share your birthday.

FEBRUARY 12

On this day in 1879: The first artificial ice rink in North America opens (Madison Square Garden, New York City).

Dive In: Over a mile of wrought-iron pipes beneath the rink circulated liquid ammonia brine to freeze water sprayed above.

Speak Up: Creating a way to preserve a bit of winter during the other seasons is a pretty cool invention. If you could preserve a part of one season in a building, what would it be and why?

_____

_____

_____

_____

_____

_____

_____

_____

_____

_____

_____

_____

Act Out: It may be wintertime but try on a bathing suit today to remind yourself that summer will return. If you have an indoor public pool in town, go for a swim!

FEBRUARY 13

On this day in 1633: Astronomer Galileo arrives in Rome to stand trial before Inquisition for saying that the Earth revolves around the sun, not the other way around.

Dive In: Many people once believed that everything revolved around the Earth. But looks can be deceiving. Galileo's studies of the heavens convinced him of a truth many people did not want to accept.

Speak Up: Have you ever struggled to tell someone the truth because you were afraid of the way they would react?

_____

_____

_____

_____

_____

_____

_____

_____

_____

_____

_____

_____

_____

Act Out: Don't be afraid of the truth. It is more valuable than ignorance or deceit.

FEBRUARY 14

On this day in 1876: Alexander Graham Bell and Elisha Gray submit separate telephone patent applications. Bell's application is processed hours before Gray's, making him the rightful patent holder.

Dive In: Elisha Gray told his lawyer on February 11 (Friday) to submit his application, but his lawyer waited until Monday, costing his client fame and fortune.

Speak Up: Have you ever lost a game or race by a point or a second? How could you have prepared differently to play better than you did?

_____

_____

_____

_____

_____

_____

_____

_____

_____

_____

_____

_____

_____

Act Out: Don't wait until tomorrow to do what you can do today. You'll never get back the time you waste!

FEBRUARY 15

On this day in 399 BC: The city of Athens sentences philosopher Socrates to death for "corrupting the minds of the young" and impiety (failure to heed the gods of Athens).
Dive In: Socrates spoke highly of Athens's enemies and poorly of well-respected citizens of Athens. He also joked during his trial that his punishment should be free meals in the finest dining hall for the rest of his life!
Speak Up: Sometimes, new ideas threaten old and cherished traditions. What is your favorite tradition at home or in your country?

_____

_____

_____

_____

_____

_____

_____

_____

_____

_____

_____

_____

_____

Act Out: Ask your parents and siblings to help you create a new family tradition. It might be a Christmas tradition, a summer tradition, or a birthday tradition. You decide!

FEBRUARY 16

On this day in 600: Pope Gregory the Great declares that the proper response to a sneeze is "God bless you."

Dive In: A plague occurred during Gregory's reign with sneezing being an early symptom of the disease. The phrase served as a prayer for healing.

Speak Up: "God bless you" is but one of many phrases said after sneezing. What do you say when someone sneezes? Why do you say that?

_____

_____

_____

_____

_____

_____

_____

_____

_____

_____

_____

_____

_____

Act Out: Next time you hear someone sneeze, try out this German phrase: Gesundheit! Pronounced *guh-**zoont**-hahyt*, it means "health".

FEBRUARY 17

On this day in 1936: The world's first superhero, the
Phantom, debuts in a newspaper cartoon strip.

Dive In: The Phantom possessed no superpowers like X-ray
vision or wall-climbing abilities, but relied on his fitness,
strength, and smarts to outwit the bad guys.

Speak Up: Superheroes fight for justice where traditional law
enforcement is outmatched. Why do you think superheroes
are so popular? Who is your favorite superhero and why?

_____

_____

_____

_____

_____

_____

_____

_____

_____

_____

_____

_____

_____

_____

_____

Act Out: Create your own superhero! Give this crimefighter
a name and one special power.

FEBRUARY 18

On this day in 1930: Elm Farm Ollie (nicknamed "Nellie Jay" and, later, "Sky Queen") becomes the first cow to fly on an airplane.

Dive In: Nellie Jay also became the first cow milked mid-flight, with her milk packaged into cardboard containers and parachuted to spectators below.

Speak Up: Food & drink delivered directly from plane to customer might sound strange, but companies today are working to do just that with drones. Do you think drone food-delivery will be successful? What problems might result from pizzas and milkshakes flying overhead?

_____

_____

_____

_____

_____

_____

_____

_____

_____

_____

Act Out: Create a slogan for a company that delivers your favorite treats by drone.

FEBRUARY 19

On this day in 1913: The first prize is included in a Cracker Jack box.

Dive In: Cracker Jack, the caramel-coated popcorn & peanut snack food, became a hit with consumers, especially at baseball games. The name of the snack food was included in the song *Take Me Out to the Ball Game*, providing free advertising for the company.

Speak Up: What's your favorite snack food? Are there some snack foods you like to eat while watching sports or movies but not at other times? How come?

_____
_____
_____
_____
_____
_____
_____
_____
_____
_____
_____
_____
_____

Act Out: Listen to the song *Take Me Out to the Ball Game*, and maybe sample some Cracker Jack while you're at it!

FEBRUARY 20

On this day in 1943: A cinder cone volcano, later named Paricutin, rises out of a farmer's cornfield near Uruapan, Mexico.

Dive In: During its nine years of activity, Paricutin damaged 90 square miles of land with ejections of rock, ash, and lava. Today, the volcano stands nearly 1,400 feet high, a dormant reminder of the power and unpredictability of nature.

Speak Up: If we think of troublesome things growing in our backyards, it's usually weeds, not volcanoes! Write down three things you would do if a volcano rose from your backyard.

_____

_____

_____

_____

_____

_____

_____

_____

_____

_____

_____

Act Out: Find the nearest volcano to your hometown. Is it dormant or active? Make a day trip to this wonder of nature!

FEBRUARY 21

On this day in 1937: The first car-airplane hybrid, nicknamed the Arrowbile, successfully flies and lands in Santa Monica, CA, USA.

Dive In: We hear so much talk about flying cars these days that we think of them as a new idea; but over 80 years ago engineers thought they were oh-so-close to developing these machines for everyday use. And yet, they failed.

Speak Up: Would you trade in your current family car for a flying car? Why or why not?

_____

_____

_____

_____

_____

_____

_____

_____

_____

_____

_____

_____

_____

_____

Act Out: Name one advantage a flying car would have over a land-based car.

FEBRUARY 22

On this day in 1920: First artificial rabbit used as a lure at a greyhound racetrack.

Dive In: O.P. Smith, the inventor of the "automatic rabbit", wanted to save jackrabbits from greyhounds and improve the public image of dog racing. Some dog tracks today don't even use fake bunnies, preferring dog bones instead.

Speak Up: Dogs hunting rabbits in the fields is one thing; dogs hunting rabbits for entertainment is another. Do you think using a stuffed animal at dog tracks is okay, or do you think all tracks should switch to dog bones? How come?

_____

_____

_____

_____

_____

_____

_____

_____

_____

Act Out: Greyhounds can't race forever, which means most are retired by the age of 5 and put up for adoption. Would a greyhound make a good pet for you? Learn three facts about greyhounds.

FEBRUARY 23

On this day in 1836: Thirteen-day Battle of the Alamo begins as the Mexican Army, led by Santa Anna, besieges the Alamo mission. Santa Anna orders the raising of a red flag, meaning no mercy will be shown.

Dive In: "Remember the Alamo!" became the rallying cry of the Texas Revolution. Forty-six days later, Santa Anna was defeated in battle and ordered his troops out of Texas.

Speak Up: Historians agree that had Santa Anna shown mercy to the Alamo independence fighters, the Texas revolution likely would have ceased. Instead, his brutality attracted many to the cause of Texas independence. Why do you think mercy is important, even when fighting a war? When you show mercy, what does that tell others about you?

_____

_____

_____

_____

_____

_____

_____

_____

_____

Act Out: Be a good sport in friendly competitions. When you win a game, don't "rub it in their face." Show mercy. Congratulate your opponent for a match well played.

FEBRUARY 24

On this day in 1942: The Battle of Los Angeles begins as anti-aircraft fire takes aim at rumored (but non-existent) Japanese warplanes in the skies.

Dive In: Five people died in the "battle" (three in car crashes and two from heart attacks) that the military later blamed on "war nerves." Apparently, a stray weather balloon led to the confusion.

Speak Up: Sometimes we let fear get the best of us and get all worked up over nothing. Have you ever mistaken something harmless for something dangerous? What was it?

_____
_____
_____
_____
_____
_____
_____
_____
_____
_____
_____

Act Out: When you feel afraid of the unknown, stop to think about what you *do* know. Does it line up with your worst fears? Probably not, which means… don't freak out!

FEBRUARY 25

On this day in 1924: Marie Boyd, high school basketball player, scores 156 points in a game.

Dive In: Boyd's team, Lonaconing Central (MD, USA) defeated rival Ursuline Academy 163-3!

Speak Up: With Boyd's team up big, one wonders why the other players only scored seven points. Do you think she should have shared the ball more with her teammates? Why or why not?

_____

_____

_____

_____

_____

_____

_____

_____

_____

_____

_____

_____

_____

_____

Act Out: Winning decisively is impressive, but there comes a point where you have nothing left to prove. A good sport never humiliates an opponent. Be a good sport!

FEBRUARY 26

On this day in 2018: The Global Seed Vault in Svalbard, Norway stores its 1 millionth seed sample.

Dive In: The Global Seed Vault is a storage facility for seeds from around the world buried inside of a mountain and kept at a constant temperature of -18º C (-40º F).

Speak Up: Ever hear the phrase "insurance policy"? An insurance policy ensures you can replace something you lose to an unexpected event. The seed vault ensures that in case of war, plague, or famine, crops from around the world can be regrown. What's the most important thing in your life that you would like to have a backup copy of? Why?

_____

_____

_____

_____

_____

_____

_____

_____

_____

_____

Act Out: Visit **https://tour.croptrust.org/** for a virtual tour of the Svalbard seed vault!

FEBRUARY 27

On this day in 1813: US Congress passes first Vaccine Act to fight the smallpox disease.

Dive In: Due to modern vaccination efforts, smallpox has been eradicated. In the 100 years prior to eradication, 500 million people died of the disease!

Speak Up: Are you afraid of getting shots? Do you think the benefits of shots (protecting you from diseases) outweighs the pain of the needle?

_____

_____

_____

_____

_____

_____

_____

_____

_____

_____

_____

_____

_____

_____

_____

Act Out: If you're afraid of getting shots because of needle pain, practice pinching yourself ahead of time. It will get you accustomed to the brief pain spike from a shot.

FEBRUARY 28

On this day in 1939: The word *dord* (meaning 'density'), accidentally included in G. and C. Meriam Co.'s *New International Dictionary*, is discovered by an editor.

Dive In: The mistake first occurred in 1934 but went unnoticed for five years. Apparently, the chemistry editor sent in a revision slip which read "D or d, density" to add the word *density* to the abbreviations list. Because the first part was typed with spaces as "D o r d" it was mistaken for a word and approved for publication.

Speak Up: *Dord* was not completely removed from the dictionary until 1947. Even though it was a mistake, do you think *dord* should be added to the English language? Why or why not?

_____

_____

_____

_____

_____

_____

_____

Act Out: Hey, mistakes happen! And this 'ghost word' escaped the notice of several highly educated editors. The next time a teacher corrects your spelling mistakes, share this story with him or her.

FEBRUARY
OUTRO

Time Capsule: _____
_____
_____
_____

I chased my dreams by: _____
_____
_____
_____

I made the world a better place by: _____
_____
_____
_____

I'm looking forward to: _____
_____
_____
_____

Next play: _____
_____

MARCH
INTRO

"*Optimism is a happiness magnet.*
If you stay positive, good things and good
people will be drawn to you."
- Mary Lou Retton

MARCH 1

On this day in 1961: US President John F. Kennedy issues an executive order establishing the Peace Corps.

Dive In: At President Kennedy's inaugural address, he famously said, "Ask not what your country can do for you, ask what you can do for your country." The Peace Corps, focused on lifting developing nations to higher living standards, exemplified that call to service.

Speak Up: Getting help can be tough if you have nothing to offer in return. Why do you think it's important to help your neighbors even if they can't give you anything tangible in return?

_____

_____

_____

_____

_____

_____

_____

_____

_____

Act Out: An old saying goes, "Give a man a fish and he'll eat for a day; teach a man to fish and he'll eat for life." Ask a friend or sibling what they want to do with their lives; ask them how you can help them achieve their goals.

MARCH 2

On this day in 1807: US Congress bans the importation of slaves into the US beginning January 1, 1808.

Dive In: This was a step toward ending slavery. However, the law did not ban the sale of people already in slavery or the sale of children born into slavery.

Speak Up: Abolitionists (people who fought to end slavery) often settled for small victories rather than holding out for big ones, but over time their small victories added up. Do you get frustrated when you don't get everything you want right now? How might you get everything you want by adding up "small victories" over time?

_____

_____

_____

_____

_____

_____

_____

_____

_____

Act Out: An old adage goes, "The journey of a thousand miles begins with a single step." When thinking about your dreams, remember that big change doesn't come overnight. You must work at it every single day!

MARCH 3

On this day in 1855: US Congress approves funding to establish the US Camel Corps.

Dive In: From 1856-1866 the US military experimented using camels in the Southwest. After the Civil War, most were sold at auction but a few dozen escaped into the wilds. The last sighting of one of these wild camels was in Arizona in 1891.

Speak Up: Would you like to ride a camel? What about an elephant? Or a horse? Write down why you would or wouldn't want to ride each of those animals.

_____

_____

_____

_____

_____

_____

_____

_____

_____

_____

Act Out: One of the US Army's camel drivers was a man named Hi Jolly. A monument to him stands in Quartzite, AZ, USA. Find a picture of the monument online.

MARCH 4

On this day in 1924: Claydon Sunny publishes the song *Happy Birthday to You.*

Dive In: Happy Birthday to You is based on the melody of an earlier song called *Good Morning to All.*

Speak Up: If today's your birthday… Happy Birthday! If not, you're probably dreaming of presents you might get. What do you want most for your birthday? How do you plan to celebrate your birthday?

_____

_____

_____

_____

_____

_____

_____

_____

_____

_____

_____

_____

_____

_____

Act Out: Bake a cake to celebrate the birthday song—it's a great excuse for a treat!

MARCH 5

On this day in 1770: British soldiers kill 5 American colonists in what comes to be known as the Boston Massacre.

Dive In: A mob was verbally abusing 8 British soldiers when men in the crowd began throwing snowballs and rocks at the soldiers. Future US President John Adams defended the soldiers in court. Six were cleared of wrongdoing, while two were convicted of manslaughter. The guilty men were branded on their thumbs with the letter 'M'.

Speak Up: Despite opposition from many of his compatriots, John Adams represented the soldiers in court. He insisted that the accused must receive a fair trial. Why is it important to treat others fairly even when you're mad at them?

_____

_____

_____

_____

_____

_____

_____

_____

Act Out: Don't take matters into your own hands when you're angry with siblings or friends. Instead, ask an adult to judge between the two of you.

MARCH 6

On this day in 1945: 3-time collegiate gymnastics champion George Nissen receives a patent for his invention, the modern trampoline.

Dive In: Nissen got the idea for the trampoline when he watched circus trapeze artists use their safety nets for additional tricks. He thought a similar device would help with his gymnastics training.

Speak Up: What's your favorite exercise or playground equipment? Why do you like that one the best? Are there any tricks you wish you could do on a trampoline that you can't do now?

_____
_____
_____
_____
_____
_____
_____
_____
_____
_____

Act Out: Come up with an idea for a piece of equipment that will help you perform better at your favorite sport.

MARCH 7

On this day in 1946: US government evacuates residents of Bikini Atoll in advance of open-air nuclear weapons testing.

Dive In: You've probably heard of bikini swimsuits, but maybe not of the Bikini Atoll. Turns out the swimsuits were named after the island when marketers wanted a flashy name for the new fashion—and what flashier name than an island where nuclear bombs were detonated?

Speak Up: Marketers spend lots of time and money choosing the perfect name for everything from breakfast cereals to the latest must-have toys. Think of a food you wanted to try, a movie you wanted to see, or a toy you wanted to buy based on its name. What was it?

_____

_____

_____

_____

_____

_____

_____

_____

Act Out: Next time you visit a restaurant, pay close attention to the names of food items on the menu—especially the desserts. Usually they have clever names that entice you buy.

MARCH 8

On this day in 2014: Malaysia Airlines flight MH370, en route to Beijing, China with 239 people onboard, disappears from the skies.

Dive In: Pieces of MH370 have washed up on shores of the Indian Ocean since the plane's disappearance, but the last hours of the flight remain a mystery.

Speak Up: Occasionally, planes crash. But flying is still safer than traveling by boat, train, or car. Are you afraid of flying in planes? Why or why not?

_____

_____

_____

_____

_____

_____

_____

_____

_____

_____

_____

Act Out: The more familiar you become with something, the less scary it seems. If you are afraid of something, learn more about it. Knowledge helps us confront and overcome our fears.

MARCH 9

Public kissing banned and deemed punishable by death in Naples, Italy.

Dive In: The public kissing ban was designed to stop the spread of a disease sweeping Europe. Italians, accustomed to greeting each other with kisses, found the ban difficult to endure.

Speak Up: Imagine a ban on public handshaking or hugging. Would you find such a ban hard to endure? Why or why not? If the ban was designed to stop the spread of a deadly disease, would you find it easier to go along with?

_____

_____

_____

_____

_____

_____

_____

_____

_____

_____

Act Out: Sometimes cultural norms (like handshaking) are best set aside to promote public health. Do your best to stop the spread of germs by covering coughs and sneezes and washing your hands.

MARCH 10

Inventor Alexander Graham Bell inadvertently places the first telephone call in history.

Dive In: While fine-tuning the invention, Bell called out to his assistant, "Mr. Watson come here, I want you." To Bell's delight, Watson made his way from an adjoining room to announce he heard Bell's words through the telephone.

Speak Up: Success can come at times when we lease expect it, even when we're frustrated with repeated failures. Do you find it hard to keep going when you aren't winning? What makes you try harder to succeed?

_____
_____
_____
_____
_____
_____
_____
_____
_____
_____
_____

Act Out: As college basketball coach Jimmy Valvano once said, "Don't give up, don't ever give up." Say those words to yourself when failure seems certain. They may save you!

MARCH 11

On this day in 2011: A 9.0 magnitude earthquake off the east coast of Japan triggers a tsunami that kills thousands.

Dive In: The tsunami traveled as far as six miles inland and completely destroyed more than 120,000 buildings.

Speak Up: An early warning system gave residents of Tokyo one minute of warning about the impending tsunami. If you had only one minute to grab precious items from your home before fleeing, what would you grab?

_____

_____

_____

_____

_____

_____

_____

_____

_____

_____

Act Out: Even when tragedies strike halfway around the world, you can make a difference. While many charities lend aid to victims of natural disasters, one good example is the American Red Cross. Visit **https://www.redcross.org/** and learn what you can do to help.

MARCH 12

On this day in 1894: Coca-Cola is bottled and sold for the first time in Vicksburg, MS, USA.

Dive In: Coca-Cola, whose name derives from the ingredients of coca leaves and kola nuts, was sold for years in pharmacies and shops by the glass before being bottled.

Speak Up: Asa Candler, the founder of the Coca-Cola Company, purchased the formula of the famous beverage from John Pemberton in 1888 for less than $2,000. Today, the company is worth more than $200 billion! Why do you think Coca-Cola became such a great success?

_____

_____

_____

_____

_____

_____

_____

_____

_____

_____

Act Out: Dreaming up a big idea and sticking with a big idea are two different things. Pledge to be more like Asa Candler than John Pemberton.

MARCH 13

On this day in 1781: Astronomer William Herschel observes a "comet" in the night sky which turns out to be the undiscovered planet Uranus.

Dive In: The heavenly bodies Uranus, Neptune, and Pluto all were mistaken for other kinds of celestial objects before being identified as planets.

Speak Up: Why do you think some people achieve what others before them tried to do and failed? Is it persistence or just plain luck?

_____

_____

_____

_____

_____

_____

_____

_____

_____

_____

_____

Act Out: Sometimes we don't see what we aren't looking for. Change your mindset. ALWAYS expect the answers to your problems are close at hand. Many important discoveries and inventions have come about this way.

MARCH 14

On this day in 1794: Eli Whitney patents the cotton gin, a machine designed to separate cotton seeds from cotton fiber.

Dive In: If you've ever picked cotton and tried to separate the seeds from fiber, you'll understand how amazing this invention is. If you've never picked cotton, thank your lucky stars. It's rotten work!

Speak Up: We often take modern marvels for granted. Cheap clothes, cheap food, and rapid transportation are a few examples. What are you thankful for that didn't exist 100 years ago?

_____

_____

_____

_____

_____

_____

_____

_____

_____

_____

_____

Act Out: Come up with an easier way to do a household chore (i.e., cleaning mirrors, folding towels, or removing pet hair from the couch)!

MARCH 15

On this day in 2018: Toy store chain Toys "R" Us announces that it will close all its stores.

Dive In: Unable to compete with online retailers and losing money for years, Toys "R" Us filed for bankruptcy. Since that time, Toys "R" Us opened two stores and now sells toys on Amazon.com.

Speak Up: Toys "R" Us used to be the biggest and best place to shop for toys. Do you like shopping for toys in a toy store or online? Why did you answer the way you did?

_____

_____

_____

_____

_____

_____

_____

_____

_____

_____

_____

_____

Act Out: Think of three attractions a toy store could use to entice kids to shop there instead of online.

MARCH 16

On this day in 1792: King Gustav III is shot at a masked ball at the Royal Opera House in Stockholm (he dies 13 days later of his wound.)

Dive In: King Gustav III was warned in a letter that a conspiracy to murder him was planned at the masked ball, but he chose to ignore the warning.

Speak Up: Why do you think the King's assassin chose to commit his crime wearing a mask in the darkness of the opera house?

_____

_____

_____

_____

_____

_____

_____

_____

_____

_____

Act Out: Take warning signs seriously. Sometimes this means recognizing "bad feelings" about certain places or situations; other times it means avoiding places and situations that aren't safe. Keep your guard up!

MARCH 17

On this day in 432: Irish pirates capture Saint Patrick from his home in Britain and take him as a slave to Ireland.

Dive In: Young Patrick spent six years a slave before escaping from his captors and returning to his family. He returned to Ireland years later as a missionary to convert the Irish to Christianity.

Speak Up: Why do you think Saint Patrick returned to the land of the people who enslaved him? Do you think it is hard to show goodness to those who have done you wrong?

_____

_____

_____

_____

_____

_____

_____

_____

_____

_____

_____

Act Out: Be slow to anger and quick to forgive. You'll feel better and earn the respect of others.

MARCH 18

On this day in 1881: The Barnum & Bailey Circus, proclaimed as "The Greatest Show on Earth," debuts at Madison Square Garden, NY, USA.

Dive In: Barnum & Bailey Circus later merged with Ringling Brothers Circus to become greater than ever. Citing declining ticket sales and animal treatment concerns, however, the circus folded up its tents in 2017.

Speak Up: Do you think it is more fun to watch animals do tricks at a circus or go about their business in enclosures at a zoo? Do you think keeping animals in circuses or zoos is cruel? Why or why not?

_____

_____

_____

_____

_____

_____

_____

_____

_____

Act Out: Keeping pets can teach us a lot about animals and ourselves! If you'd like to own a pet, educate yourself about that animal before buying it. If you do own a pet, always remember that animal depends on you!

MARCH 19

On this day in 1775: Four family members are buried in a stable beneath an avalanche for 37 days.

Dive In: Three of the four family members survived, while the youngest (a six-year-old boy) died. The survivors lived on a small amount of walnuts and milk from a surviving goat.

Speak Up: Do you think you could survive trapped under a mountain of snow for 37 days? What might you do to keep yourself from going bored or crazy?

_____

_____

_____

_____

_____

_____

_____

_____

_____

_____

Act Out: Nothing can prepare us for such an ordeal as being buried in an avalanche. But the next time you are bored out of your mind, think about all the good things you have to be thankful for!

MARCH 20

On this day in 1345: Scholars at the University of Paris believe that a triple-conjunction in the heavens of Mars, Jupiter, and Saturn creates the Black Death plague that sweeps Europe.

Dive In: Rats carrying fleas were the likely spreader of the plague, with a catastrophic death toll for the continent.

Speak Up: Some people put a lot of faith in the movement of the stars and planets (astrology). Do you believe the position of the stars and planets can affect your life, or do you think it's a bunch of hocus-pocus? Why?

_____

_____

_____

_____

_____

_____

_____

_____

_____

_____

_____

Act Out: Scientists constantly discover things that affect our lives, but one thing is certain: the choices YOU make will have the greatest effect on your life. Choose wisely!

MARCH 21

On this day in 1962: A bear named Yogi becomes the first creature test-ejected from an airplane flying at supersonic speeds.

Dive In: The key word here is *test.* Seven years earlier, pilot George F. Smith ejected from his aircraft at 777 mph after the controls failed. The injuries he sustained convinced the Air Force to test ejection seats during supersonic flights on non-humans. Thankfully, Yogi fared better than George.

Speak Up: Do you think it is okay to put an animal through a test of this kind if the result might save the lives of people? Why or why not?

_____

_____

_____

_____

_____

_____

_____

_____

_____

_____

Act Out: No matter how good an idea looks on paper, it can result in real-life danger. Think about that the next time you have a bright idea that hasn't been tested by experts.

MARCH 22

On this day in 2018: New research estimates 1.8 trillion pieces of plastic swirl in the "Pacific Trash Vortex" between Japan and California.

Dive In: The Pacific Trash Vortex, also known as the Great Pacific Garbage Patch, consists of marine debris and litter swirling in the ocean. Plastic doesn't biodegrade, it only breaks into smaller pieces, making clean up a monumental task.

Speak Up: When you throw away a piece of plastic, do you know where it goes? If you litter, what do you think happens to that garbage?

_____
_____
_____
_____
_____
_____
_____
_____
_____
_____

Act Out: Cleaning up the Pacific Ocean is too great a job for a single person but cleaning up your neighborhood is not. Grab a trash bag and pick up any litter on your street.

MARCH 23

On this day in 1775: Virginia statesman Patrick Henry declares in a speech, "Give me liberty or give me death!"

Dive In: Known best for his speech-making, Patrick Henry turned down President Washington's offers to serve as Secretary of State and Supreme Court Justice. He also declined overtures to run for President when Washington opted not to seek a third term.

Speak Up: Henry's popularity among the people increased the more he resisted power. Do you trust someone more who is reluctant to lead over someone who is very eager to take charge? Why or why not?

_____

_____

_____

_____

_____

_____

_____

_____

_____

Act Out: Being a leader is about how you can serve others best, not about being perceived as the best. Remember that as you make your mark on the world!

MARCH 24

On this day in 2019: Investigation into the 2016 US election by Special Counsel Robert Mueller finds no evidence of collusion between President Donald Trump and Russia.

Dive In: National elections should be free from influence by foreign governments, but that doesn't mean foreign governments don't try to interfere.

Speak Up: Countries are like families. How would you react if someone showed up at your door telling your family what they should eat for dinner, who they should be friends with, or where they should shop?

_____

_____

_____

_____

_____

_____

_____

_____

_____

_____

Act Out: In democratic forms of government, voting is a cherished right. The next time you have a vote or say in a matter, remember that what you believe trumps what other people say you should believe.

MARCH 25

Residents of Innisfail, Australia make an 8km-long banana split, the world's largest.

Dive In: Bananas are a major cash crop in the region, so it seems fitting that the world's largest banana split would be made there. Hundreds of volunteers laid out 40,000 bananas end-to-end and covered them with ice cream and toppings. Yum!

Speak Up: If you want to break this world record, you'll need lots of help! What dessert treat would you like to make bigger and better than any in world history?

_____

_____

_____

_____

_____

_____

_____

_____

_____

_____

_____

Act Out: Find out the world record for your dessert treat choice. How much would it cost to break the record?

MARCH 26

On this day in 1953: Dr. Jonas Salk announces successful test of his vaccine against poliomyelitis, the virus that causes polio.

Dive In: Polio was a widespread disease in the 20th century that primarily affected children. However, older people were affected, too, such as US President Franklin Roosevelt who was crippled by the disease at age 39.

Speak Up: 1.8 million school children participated as guinea pigs in the testing of Salk's vaccine. Would you participate in a such a test if you didn't know the vaccine was safe? Why or why not?

_____

_____

_____

_____

_____

_____

_____

_____

_____

_____

Act Out: New diseases arise all the time and devastate communities around the world. If you would like to find cures, you might pursue a career in science or medicine.

MARCH 27

On this day in 1980: Mount St. Helens volcano in WA, USA erupts after 123 years of dormancy, culminating in a major eruption on May 18th, 1980.

Dive In: The May 1980 eruption was the worst volcanic eruption in US history, killing 57 people, including innkeeper Harry Truman, who was buried beneath the exploding mountain with his many cats and pink Cadillac.

Speak Up: 83-year-old Harry Truman (not the former US President) refused to leave his residence despite many urging him to do so. If a natural disaster threatened your home, would you refuse to leave, or grab what you could and scram?

_____

_____

_____

_____

_____

_____

_____

_____

_____

_____

Act Out: We all treasure our homes, but a home is nothing without you! Harry chose Mount St. Helens as his hill to die on, but it didn't have to be that way.

MARCH 28

On this day in 845: 5,000 Viking raiders led by Ragnar Lodbrok besiege the city of Paris.

Dive In: Paris and Viking raiders seem too incongruous to be real, and yet it happened. The Viking raiders departed only after receiving 83,000 ounces of gold and silver from the Frankish King, Charles the Bald.

Speak Up: Viking war parties assaulted Paris for nearly 50 years before the event of 845. How would you defend your home if it were hit by continued vandalism and break-ins?

_____

_____

_____

_____

_____

_____

_____

_____

_____

_____

Act Out: The Vikings took advantage of Frankish civil wars to invade Paris. Realize that when you argue with family and friends, unscrupulous people may try to undermine you for their own ends.

MARCH 29

On this day in 1795: Ludwig van Beethoven, aged 24, performs his own piano concertos publicly for the first time (Vienna, Austria).

Dive In: Beethoven first performed before an audience at age 7 when his musically driven father sought to promote him as a child prodigy in the same vein as Mozart.

Speak Up: Beethoven was a master composer, but he wasn't born with his skills. He developed them under harsh training over two decades before his debut. Do you think you are destined to do some thing or another? How hard will you work to be the best at what you want to do?

_____

_____

_____

_____

_____

_____

_____

_____

_____

Act Out: When you watch someone perform better than all the rest, realize they are not "gifted" or "talented." Rather, they trained harder than all the rest for years or decades to become as good as they are. You can too, if you're willing!

MARCH 30

Halley's Comet first recorded passage of Earth by Chinese astronomers.

Dive In: Halley's Comet (named after Edmond Halley, who observed the object in 1717 and predicted its return 76 years later) was initially mistaken for a nebula.

Speak Up: Lights in the heavens have been treated as ominous signs for time immemorial. Do you think a comet portends good or bad things to come or is it just a natural event to be enjoyed?

_____

_____

_____

_____

_____

_____

_____

_____

_____

_____

_____

_____

_____

Act Out: Familiarize yourself with some of the planets and constellations in the night sky.

MARCH 31

On this day in 1889: The Eiffel Tower is dedicated in Paris, France.

Dive In: Bridge-builder Gustave Eiffel, who designed the Eiffel Tower, was a skilled craftsman of metal structures. He also designed the metal framework of the Statue of Liberty.

Speak Up: What is your favorite material to make arts and crafts out of (i.e., Legos, cardboard, wood, paint, etc.)? Why do you prefer that material to other types?

_____
_____
_____
_____
_____
_____
_____
_____
_____
_____
_____
_____

Act Out: Take your favorite material for arts & crafts and build/draw a replica of the Eiffel Tower.

MARCH
OUTRO

Time Capsule: _____

_____

_____

_____

I chased my dreams by: _____

_____

_____

_____

I made the world a better place by: _____

_____

_____

_____

I'm looking forward to: _____

_____

_____

_____

Next play: _____

_____

APRIL
INTRO

> *"Our greatest weakness lies in giving up.*
> *The most certain way to succeed is always*
> *to try just one more time."*
>
> – Thomas Edison

APRIL 1

On this day in 1928: Louis Marx introduces his toy company's wildly successful yo-yo.

Dive In: Who would've thought a disk on a string could be so much fun? The first known yo-yo was made in Greece over 2,500 years ago, but when Louis Marx produced quality versions at a cheap price in the US, sales skyrocketed. In fact, his toy company sold about 100 million yo-yos in the 1920's!

Speak Up: What is your favorite toy to play with that doesn't require electricity or batteries? What makes that toy so much fun to play with?

_____

_____

_____

_____

_____

_____

_____

_____

_____

Act Out: Yo-yo users have developed many tricks for the toy. Two popular ones are "walk the dog" and "the elevator." Grab a yo-yo and learn these tricks!

APRIL 2

On this day in 1878: US President Rutherford B. Hayes opens the South Lawn to the public for the first Easter egg rolling event at the White House.

Dive In: Rolling colorfully dyed eggs on Easter has a long tradition, perhaps going back a thousand years or more.

Speak Up: What Easter traditions, if any, do you celebrate at home? Have you ever dyed or rolled eggs for fun?

_____

_____

_____

_____

_____

_____

_____

_____

_____

_____

_____

_____

_____

_____

Act Out: With your parent's permission, try dyeing a hard-boiled egg with food coloring. How colorful can you make your egg?

APRIL 3

On this day in 1860: The Pony Express begins service between St. Joseph, MO and Sacramento, CA, USA.

Dive In: The Pony Express was a mail-delivery service operated by horse riders. It only lasted about 18 months before the transcontinental telegraph made it obsolete.

Speak Up: Today, e-mail has made even the postal service largely obsolete... at least for sending messages. Besides messages, what might you send by the postal service?

_____

_____

_____

_____

_____

_____

_____

_____

_____

_____

_____

_____

_____

_____

Act Out: Send a postcard or letter to a friend or family member... or even yourself. Don't forget the stamp!

APRIL 4

On this day in 1841: US President William Henry Harrison dies 31 days after being sworn into office.

Dive In: President Harrison likely died of typhoid contracted from polluted water in Washington, D.C. His 31-day presidency was the shortest in US history.

Speak Up: 31 days isn't a lot of time to accomplish everything you want to do in life, but what if you knew you only had 31 days to live? What would you do?

_____

_____

_____

_____

_____

_____

_____

_____

_____

_____

_____

_____

_____

_____

Act Out: Make a calendar for the rest of the month and write down one thing you want to do that day. You'll be surprised how much you accomplish in a short time!

APRIL 5

On this day in 1722: Dutch explorer Jacob Roggeveen discovers Easter Island (named for the day of discovery.)

Dive In: The remote island off the coast of South America is best known for its ancient stone statues with giant heads, called Mo'ai. The ancient inhabitants of the island created about 900 such statues, including one that was 69 feet tall!

Speak Up: For an island people, the Mo'ai sculptures are a remarkable achievement. Why do you think a small community would expend so much effort to create them?

_____

_____

_____

_____

_____

_____

_____

_____

_____

_____

_____

_____

Act Out: Find a picture of an Easter Island Mo'ai at the library or online. Paint your own picture of it!

APRIL 6

The first Hollywood feature film is shown on an airplane (*The Lost World*, based on Arthur Conan Doyle's novel.)

Dive In: Today, airplane trips lack no shortage of in-flight entertainment with a vast selection of movies and TV episodes available on demand.

Speak Up: What type of entertainment would you enjoy on an airplane? Movies, books, video games, or maybe a game of cards? What's a kind of in-flight entertainment that would be cool, but airlines don't offer?

_____

_____

_____

_____

_____

_____

_____

_____

_____

_____

_____

_____

Act Out: Put Arthur Conan Doyle's book *The Lost World* on your reading list.

APRIL 7

On this day in 30: Probable date of Jesus' crucifixion in Jerusalem.

Dive In: The crucifixion may have happened as late as the year 33, but due to ancient record keeping no one knows for sure.

Speak Up: Jesus' crucifixion is one of the most consequential events in human history. Nearly 2,000 years later, billions of people still look to His life as a guide. When you pass away, what do you want people to remember about you?

_____

_____

_____

_____

_____

_____

_____

_____

_____

_____

_____

_____

Act Out: Live your life the way you want to be remembered.

APRIL 8

On this day in 1766: The first fire escape is patented.

Dive In: The contraption consisted of a large wicker basket attached to a chain and pulley system designed to allow the fire escapee to lower him or herself to safety.

Speak Up: The contraption sounds dangerous, but not as dangerous as a house fire. How would you safely escape your home in case of a fire?

_____
_____
_____
_____
_____
_____
_____
_____
_____
_____
_____
_____
_____
_____

Act Out: Work with your family members to develop an escape plan in case of a fire. Think carefully about any tools you might need to aid in your escape.

APRIL 9

On this day in 1865: Confederate General Robert E. Lee and more than 26,000 troops under his command surrender to Union forces in Appomattox, VA, USA.

Dive In: Gen. Lee was in retreat, hoping to reach the railroad depot in Appomattox where he might transport his soldiers further south to join the Army of Tennessee. Federal troops, however, blocked their escape.

Speak Up: Some soldiers vow to fight to the last breath, while others surrender when they've been bested. Out-gunned, out-manned, and out-maneuvered, do you think General Lee was right to surrender, or should he and his men have fought to the end? Why?

_____

_____

_____

_____

_____

_____

_____

_____

_____

_____

Act Out: Showing humility means admitting when you're wrong. Own up to your wrongs and your defeats.

APRIL 10

On this day in 2019: Astronomers release the first-ever radio wave image of a black hole.

Dive In: Nothing can escape a black hole, not even light. So how did astronomers take a picture of one? Technically, they captured the bright ring of light around the black hole formed as light bends into it.

Speak Up: Some physicists think black holes might be "wormholes" that lead to other universes, while some think they may lead to the end of time. What do you think happens to everything that falls inside a black hole?

_____

_____

_____

_____

_____

_____

_____

_____

_____

_____

Act Out: Objects falling into black holes are stretched into strands of atoms, a process called "spaghettification". Paint a picture of something getting "spaghettified"!

APRIL 11

On this day in 1973: Apollo 13 lunar mission launches, aborts Moon landing 2 days later when oxygen tank fails.

Dive In: We often think of the glories of space travel, but not of the dangers. Thankfully, mission control devised a plan to safely bring the astronauts back to Earth.

Speak Up: The astronauts didn't get a chance to walk on the Moon, but they did get a chance to live another day. Do you think their mission was a success? Why or why not? What can we learn about ourselves when everything goes wrong?

_____

_____

_____

_____

_____

_____

_____

_____

_____

_____

_____

Act Out: Planning what to do when everything goes wrong is as important as planning what to do when everything goes as right. Always have a backup plan!

APRIL 12

On this day in 2016: Scientists and business leaders unveil the *Breakthrough Starshot* initiative to launch wafer-sized spacecraft to the nearest star system, Alpha Centauri.

Dive In: The plan involves technology not yet invented, but realistic in the near future. Ground-based lasers would propel the spacecraft on a "lightsail" at 100 million miles per hour!

Speak Up: The lightsail technology would enable spacecraft to reach Alpha Centauri in 20 years. Pictures beamed back would take over 4 years to reach Earth. What value is there in undertaking a mission of this kind?

_____

_____

_____

_____

_____

_____

_____

_____

_____

_____

Act Out: Want to learn more about *Breakthrough Starshot*? Visit **https://breakthroughinitiatives.org/initiative/3** to track the progress and share your ideas!

APRIL 13

On this day in 1992: Crystal Pepsi debuts in 5 test markets across the US.

Dive In: Cola is supposed to be brown, right? Well, in the 1990's, Pepsi decided to launch a clear cola beverage to capitalize on the public's interest in purity. It was a success! But rival Coke introduced a "kamikaze" clear cola that was sugar-free to intentionally confuse the public about what was (or wasn't) in Crystal Pepsi. Both products were ruined.

Speak Up: Sometimes color makes us think differently about things. Would you drink green milk or eat pink hamburgers even if they smelled okay? Why or why not?

_____

_____

_____

_____

_____

_____

_____

_____

_____

_____

Act Out: This is an easy one—go read *Green Eggs and Ham* by Dr. Seuss. What's the moral of the story?

APRIL 14

On this day in 1912: The RMS Titanic ocean liner, on her maiden voyage, strikes an iceberg in the North Atlantic and sinks.

Dive In: Due to the size of the ship and state-of-the-art safety designs, many considered the Titanic unsinkable.

Speak Up: Too few lifeboats were available for all the passengers, and those lifeboats were lowered at less than capacity, leading to the deaths of over 1,500 passengers. Would you give up a seat on a lifeboat for someone else? Why or why not?

_____

_____

_____

_____

_____

_____

_____

_____

_____

Act Out: Scottish poet Robert Burns once wrote, "The best laid schemes of mice and men oft go awry." When we think we can't fail, our failure seems all the more spectacular. So, be ambitious in your plans, cautious in your expectations, and humble in your successes.

APRIL 15

On this day in 1865: US President Abraham Lincoln dies from gunshot wound suffered the night before at Ford's Theater in Washington, D.C.

Dive In: Lincoln's assassin, John Wilkes Booth, planned with several confederates to kill the Vice President and Secretary of State that same night. Only Booth succeeded.

Speak Up: Booth was a sympathizer with the Confederacy who could not accept its defeat in the War of Rebellion. Have you ever had a hard time accepting defeat? How did you react?

_____

_____

_____

_____

_____

_____

_____

_____

_____

_____

Act Out: Just because you hurt on the inside doesn't mean you should hurt others. Increasing pain can never take away pain. Talk to others about your heartbreak or sadness. It takes time to heal deep wounds.

APRIL 16

On this day in 2012: For just the 10th time in history, no Pulitzer Prize awarded for fiction.

Dive In: The Pulitzer Prize dates to 1917, so this happens about every ten years. If the panel of judges decides that no work meets its standards, then no prize is awarded.

Speak Up: Do you think a fiction book should win the Pulitzer Prize every year, even if it's only "pretty good", or do you think the judges were right to uphold their highest standards by withholding the prize?

_____

_____

_____

_____

_____

_____

_____

_____

_____

_____

_____

Act Out: Taking a 1st Place award is a great honor in any area of life, but there's no shame in 2nd Place, 3rd Place… or, just trying your best! Your consistent effort over time defines you more than a single competition.

APRIL 17

On this day in 1865: The British Library purchases the St. Cuthbert Gospel, the oldest surviving European book in its original binding.

Dive In: The St. Cuthbert Gospel is an 8th-century leather-bound pocket-sized copy of the Gospel of St. John in Latin. Through fundraising efforts, the library purchased the book for £9 million, or about USD 11,750,000!

Speak Up: The thing about rare artifacts is that they don't make them anymore! Do you like to collect old or rare things like coins or stamps? What's the most precious possession you own? Why does it mean so much to you?

_____

_____

_____

_____

_____

_____

_____

_____

_____

_____

Act Out: If you value something, you must take special care of it. This is true for objects as well as people and relationships.

APRIL 18

On this day in 1775: Paul Revere and William Dawes ride on horseback from Charlestown to Lexington, warning patriots along the way that British troops are advancing.

Dive In: Revere and Dawes alerted as many as 40 other riders to carry the message of British troop movements to patriots far and wide. The advance warning allowed the colonial militia to take up positions and defeat the British at the battles of Lexington and Concord.

Speak Up: In today's world, sirens, airhorns, and emergency broadcasts alert us to danger. How would you alert your friends and neighbors if a dangerous situation arose?

_____

_____

_____

_____

_____

_____

_____

_____

_____

_____

Act Out: If you were separated from your family in an emergency, would you know what to do? Talk to your family about places to meet and ways to get in touch.

APRIL 19

On this day in 1897: John McDermott wins the first Boston Marathon in a time of 2:55:10. McDermott's time bested the 1896 Olympic marathon time and was likely a world record.

Dive In: Marathons today are standardized at 26.2 miles. The fastest time ever recorded on a "record-eligible" course is 2:01:39, set by Eliud Kipchoge of Kenya in Berlin, 2018.

Speak Up: Runners keep running faster and faster. In fact, the top-ten marathon times have all occurred since 2014. Do you think humans are getting faster, or do you think runners are training better? Explain your answer.

_____

_____

_____

_____

_____

_____

_____

_____

_____

Act Out: Footwear is important for running, too, but not for everyone. At the 1980 Olympics in Rome, Abebe Bikila of Ethiopia won gold and set a world record... barefoot! Try running barefoot, then with shoes. Which do you prefer?

APRIL 20

On this day in 1918: Baron Manfred von Richthofen (a.k.a., the "Red Baron") shoots down his 79th & 80th plane of WWI. He is killed in action the next day.

Dive In: Richthofen originally served as a cavalryman in the German army but transferred to the Air Service when his regiment was dismounted. Reinvigorated with his new duties, he became one of the top fighter pilots of all time, both respected and feared by opposing militaries.

Speak Up: Times change. Technology advances. Supplies run out. If the hobby you love best (i.e., soccer, chess, playing piano, etc.) was no longer an option for you, how would you reinvent yourself?

_____

_____

_____

_____

_____

_____

_____

_____

Act Out: You may already be a master of (or pretty darn good at) a sport or musical instrument. In addition to these, try your hand at a completely different hobby. You may surprise yourself how good you are!

APRIL 21

On this day in 753 BC: Twin brothers Romulus and Remus, abandoned at birth and raised by wolves, establish the city of Rome.

Dive In: Where truth bleeds into myth in the Romulus & Remus tale is a matter of debate, but most accounts tell of the boys rising against a cruel king (who is their uncle) and restoring their grandfather to the throne.

Speak Up: Many cities have important histories or legends associated with their origins. Does your hometown have any legend or great historical event associated with it?

_____

_____

_____

_____

_____

_____

_____

_____

_____

_____

Act Out: Maybe nothing legendary ever happened in your city. Well, now is your chance to change that! Write a myth about the founding of your hometown.

APRIL 22

On this day in 1884: Thomas Stevens begins the first bicycle trip around the world.

Dive In: Stevens's trip began in San Francisco, CA, USA and ended over 2 ½ years later in Yokohama, Japan on December 17, 1886.

Speak Up: Stevens set out with no other purpose than to see the world by bicycle. If you could travel the world by one form of transportation, what would it be? Why?

_____

_____

_____

_____

_____

_____

_____

_____

_____

_____

_____

Act Out: Sometimes when we think about faster forms of transportation, we lose sight of the splendor of the journey. Remember, the destination isn't always the best part of the trip… often it's the journey!

APRIL 23

On this day in 1516: Bavaria adopts the Munich beer purity law of 1487, stating that only three ingredients may be used in the production of beer: water, barley, and hops.

Dive In: The law reflected concerns, in part, that brewers might use baker's grains (such as wheat and rye) and increase the cost of bread.

Speak Up: Food purity is a good thing (just try pronouncing some of the ingredients in a loaf of bread at your grocery store). But knowing the ingredients is also a matter of health, due to the allergies of some consumers. Do you think food and beverage makers should be allowed to keep their ingredients and recipes secret?

_____

_____

_____

_____

_____

_____

_____

Act Out: Even if you know the ingredients of a food, you may not be able to reproduce the recipe. Look at the ingredients of your favorite store-bought cookie and see if you can make it at home.

APRIL 24

On this day in 1898: Due to conflict surrounding Cuba's bid for independence, Spain declares war on the United States of America.

Dive In: The US prevailed in the war. In the Treaty of Paris signed later that year, Spain ceded its island possessions of Puerto Rico, Guam, and the Philippines to the US.

Speak Up: As a US territory, Puerto Rico maintains close relations to the US. However, not all citizens of Puerto Rico are convinced of the wisdom of becoming a US state. Do you think Puerto Rico should become the 51st US state?

_____

_____

_____

_____

_____

_____

_____

_____

_____

_____

_____

Act Out: To answer the question above, you will need to understand the history of Puerto Rico. Using the library or Internet, learn more about Puerto Rico.

APRIL 25

On this day in 1516: The name "America" (for the lands of the American continents) first used by German cartographer Martin Waldseemüller on his world map.

Dive In: Waldseemüller presumed the name "America" in use at the time related to Amerigo Vespucci, but some reject his assessment. Rather, they argue the American continents received their name from the Mayan name for a Nicaraguan mountain range… the "Amerrique".

Speak Up: Amerrique (also *Amerrisque*) in the Mayan language means "land of the wind." Do you think it matters where the name "America" came from? Why or why not?

_____

_____

_____

_____

_____

_____

_____

_____

_____

Act Out: Sometimes names stick, and we forget where they came from. If you don't know the meaning of your name, look it up. Does the meaning of your name define you?

APRIL 26

On this day in 1986: A nuclear reactor explosion at the Chernobyl Nuclear Power Plant (Ukraine, formerly of the USSR) casts radioactive contaminants into the environment.

Dive In: Authorities evacuated nearly 120,000 people within a 30 km radius of the power plant. The contamination spread further than that, however, leading to increased childhood thyroid cancer in the years following the disaster.

Speak Up: Living in a toxin-free environment is key to living a healthy life. Do you see pollution where you live, like dirty air or dirty water? What steps can you take to clean up the place you live?

_____
_____
_____
_____
_____
_____
_____
_____
_____
_____

Act Out: Indoor air quality is as important as outdoor air quality. Vacuuming and dusting regularly, along with a clean furnace filter, improves your air quality at home.

APRIL 27

On this day in 1865: The Mississippi steamboat *Sultana*, greatly overloaded with Union troops returning home from the Civil War, explodes, blazes, and sinks into the river.

Dive In: Historians blame a poorly repaired boiler, strained by swift river currents and excessive passenger weight, for the explosion. At least 1,181 passengers died, making the *Sultana* the worst maritime disaster in US history.

Speak Up: How would you keep yourself safe at a large indoor gathering? Would you look for exit signs, fire alarms and extinguishers, and exit stairs? Would you have a plan if you had to evacuate a building? Why is it a good idea to think about these safety measures before you need them?

_____

_____

_____

_____

_____

_____

_____

_____

_____

Act Out: Don't do something just because everybody else is doing it. If you think a situation might be unsafe, trust your instincts.

APRIL 28

On this day in 1947: Norwegian explorer Thor Heyerdahl and crew of the *Kon-Tiki* set sail from Peru to Polynesia.

Dive In: Heyerdahl believed South Americans in pre-Columbian times sailed to Polynesia. To prove it, he built a raft using old techniques. After sailing 101 days and over 4,300 miles, the Kon-Tiki successfully reached the Tuamotu Islands.

Speak Up: Heyerdahl didn't prove South Americans sailed to Polynesia long ago, but he did prove they could have done it. If Polynesians didn't arrive on their islands by boat, then how did they get there? If they got there by boat, why couldn't South Americans have done the same?

_____

_____

_____

_____

_____

_____

_____

_____

_____

Act Out: Sometimes an impossible problem only seems that way because we make the problem more difficult than it needs to be. Look for the simplest solution to your problems.

APRIL 29

On this day in 1865: Peter Roget's synonym dictionary, *Roget's Thesaurus*, first published.

Dive In: *Roget's Thesaurus* wasn't the 1st synonym dictionary published but it was the most robust, having taken 50 years to compile and perfect. Today, it remains the most widely used version in the English language.

Speak Up: Have you ever found yourself at a loss for words? What techniques might you use to work out what you want to say?

_____

_____

_____

_____

_____

_____

_____

_____

_____

_____

_____

Act Out: If you don't own a thesaurus, consider adding one to your bookshelf. Not only can it help you find the right word, but it will expand your vocabulary, too!

APRIL 30

On this day in 1888: A freak hailstorm in Moradabad, India kills 230 people and 1,600 sheep and goats.

Dive In: This was no ordinary hailstorm as the hailstones were said to be as large as oranges and blanketed some areas up to 2 feet deep!

Speak Up: How would you protect yourself from a freak hailstorm? What items in the environment might offer you protection?

_____

_____

_____

_____

_____

_____

_____

_____

_____

_____

_____

_____

_____

_____

_____

Act Out: Freeze an orange to gauge the size and hardness of the hailstones that pummeled Moradabad.

APRIL
OUTRO

Time Capsule: _____
_____
_____
_____

I chased my dreams by: _____
_____
_____
_____

I made the world a better place by: _____
_____
_____
_____

I'm looking forward to: _____
_____
_____
_____

Next play: _____
_____

MAY
INTRO

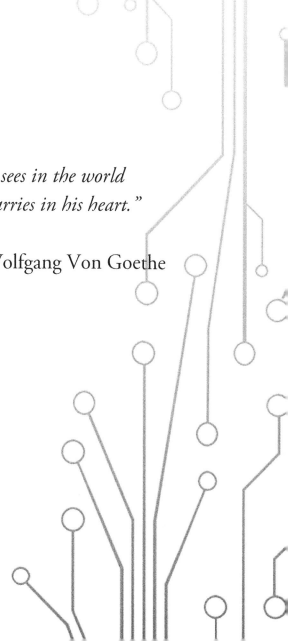

*"A man sees in the world
what he carries in his heart."*

– Johann Wolfgang Von Goethe

MAY 1

On this day in 1795: King Kamehameha of Hawai'i (the Big Island) defeats Kalanikupule and the island of O'ahu in the Battle of Nu'uanu.

Dive In: Kamehameha's decisive victory brought all the islands of Hawai'i (except for Kaua'i) under his dominion.

Speak Up: Today, Hawaiians think of themselves as a common people group, but before King Kamehameha they identified according to their islands of origin. In the same way, Americans think of themselves as a people group, but before the Civil War they identified according to their home states. How do you identify yourself? Is it by country, ethnicity, religion, or some other group? Or, do you simply see yourself as a human being?

_____

_____

_____

_____

_____

_____

_____

Act Out: How we identify ourselves affects how we live and how we view the world. No matter how you identify, try to see other people's points of view.

MAY 2

On this day in 1780: Astronomer William Herschel discovers the first binary star system, Alula Australis, located in the constellation Ursa Major (the Great Bear).

Dive In: Before Herschel's observation, stars were thought to occur apart from other stars, like singleton children. What he proved, however, is that sometimes stars are "twins".

Speak Up: Are you a twin? Have you ever wished you were a twin? Name three things you could do if you had a twin who looked just like you?

_____

_____

_____

_____

_____

_____

_____

_____

_____

Act Out: Perhaps the most famous binary star system is in the Big Dipper asterism. The Mizar and Alcor system (representing the second to last point in the handle of the Big Dipper) was used by ancient Arabs as an eyesight test. If you could discern the two stars, you were deemed to have good vision. Test your vision tonight with the Big Dipper!

MAY 3

On this day in 2000: Dave Ulmer places the first GPS-located cache off S. Fellows Road in Estacada, OR, USA.

Dive In: A cache is a waterproof container holding small trinkets, a logbook, and other items. The cache is found using a GPS receiver or similar handheld device. Ulmer is often credited with starting the outdoor game known as *geocaching*.

Speak Up: Scavenger hunt games like this have been around for ages. Ulmer brought it into the Internet age. What items would be fun to put in a cache for somebody else to find?

_____

_____

_____

_____

_____

_____

_____

_____

_____

_____

Act Out: A cache is sort of like a time capsule that you bury in the ground (though usually dug up quickly). Bury a cache of items in your yard and dig it up next May 3rd!

MAY 4

On this day in 1893: Texas rodeo cowboy Bill Picket wrestles a steer to the ground by its horns and bites its lip, inadvertently creating the sport known as *bulldogging*.

Dive In: The way Bill Picket tells it, he leapt on an unruly steer after it tried to gore his horse. You might think this dangerous sport would cost Picket his life but ironically, he died in 1932 after being kicked by a *horse*.

Speak Up: Do you think bulldogging sounds like a fun sport, or do you think it's cruel to use animals that way? What about wrestling your pet dog in the backyard? Explain your answer.

_____

_____

_____

_____

_____

_____

_____

_____

Act Out: Playing games is fun if the participants *agree* to play. Be mindful of respecting others if you plan to play a practical joke on them. They might not think it's so funny. They might get really mad!

MAY 5

On this day in 1930: English pilot Amy Johnson flies solo from London to Australia—the first woman to do so.

Dive In: Trailblazers like Johnson are known for pushing the limits of what people may achieve when they set their minds to it.

Speak Up: Have you ever been told you couldn't do something because you're too young, too small, too dumb, too slow, too inexperienced, or too lazy? How did it make you feel about your ability to achieve?

_____

_____

_____

_____

_____

_____

_____

_____

_____

_____

Act Out: We aren't always prepared enough, experienced enough, or supplied enough to achieve our dreams, but that doesn't mean we can't give chase. Often, the preparation, experience, and supplies we lack are gained in the pursuit of our dreams. Be realistic but don't make excuses not to begin!

MAY 6

On this day in 1937: German airship *Hindenburg* catches fire and explodes during docking maneuvers in NJ, USA.
Dive In: 35 of 97 people on board perished in the blast. The era of airship travel essentially ended after this disaster as the public lost confidence in the safety of the industry.
Speak Up: Only a few dozen airships remain in operation today, but they might make a comeback as cargo vessels of the future. Given the fate of the *Hindenburg*, do you think this is a bad idea, or do you trust the industry to operate cargo airships safely? Explain your answer.

_____

_____

_____

_____

_____

_____

_____

_____

_____

_____

_____

Act Out: The *Hindenburg* was a rigid airship, while blimps (like the *Goodyear* blimp) are non-rigid airships. Find out what the difference between the two is.

MAY 7

On this day in 1914: Anna Jarvis's efforts lead the US
Congress to pass a law establishing the second Sunday in
May as Mother's Day.

Dive In: Jarvis soured to the commercialization of Mother's
Day. She wanted Mother's Day celebrated from the heart,
not the department store. She said, *"A printed card means
nothing except that you are too lazy to write to the woman who
has done more for you than anyone in the world."*

Speak Up: Do you agree with Anna Jarvis that a printed
Mother's Day card shows laziness? Why or why not?

_____

_____

_____

_____

_____

_____

_____

_____

_____

_____

Act Out: Jarvis preferred the white carnation as the symbol
of Mother's Day. This Mother's Day write your mom a
handwritten note and make a "carnation" from tissue paper.

MAY 8

On this day in 1945: War-weary Allies celebrate V-E Day (Victory in Europe) as Germany signs an unconditional surrender, ending WWII on the continent.

Dive In: The end of WWII remained several months away, but after six years of hostilities the Allies sensed total victory was within reach.

Speak Up: What's the worst thing that's ever happened to you? Was there a time when you felt you wouldn't overcome it? What changed?

_____

_____

_____

_____

_____

_____

_____

_____

_____

_____

_____

Act Out: If the "worst thing" is ongoing, remember that hope and belief in victory are two very powerful weapons against the darkness. Focus on the light within you!

MAY 9

On this day in 2019: 72-year-old French adventurer Jean-Jacques Savin successfully crosses the Atlantic Ocean in a big orange barrel.

Dive In: Savin began his 4-month journey from the Canary Islands (Africa), riding the ocean currents west to the Caribbean. He survived on fresh-caught fish and a few rations stowed in the barrel.

Speak Up: Just when you thought every crazy idea had been tried, here comes Savin! What do you think the hardest part of spending 4 months asea in barrel would be? Loneliness? Boredom? Seasickness? Explain your answer.

_____

_____

_____

_____

_____

_____

_____

Act Out: Like Thor Heyerdahl, Savin hypothesized an "impossible" goal could be achieved with simple tools. Unlike Columbus, Savin didn't wait for a nation to fund his journey across the Atlantic. Rather than thinking about a fleet of ships with large crews and abundant supplies, he kept it simple and made his mark on history.

MAY 10

On this day in 1869: A ceremonial golden spike is driven into the final tie of the first transcontinental railroad at Promontory Summit, Utah Territory, USA.

Dive In: The transcontinental railroad connected the east and west extents of the American continent, forever changing the era of westward expansion.

Speak Up: The golden spike, made of over 14 troy ounces of gold and valued today about USD 26,000, was immediately removed after being driven to prevent it from being stolen. Do you think it's important to hold ceremonies at the end of big projects or accomplishments? Why or why not?

_____

_____

_____

_____

_____

_____

_____

_____

_____

_____

Act Out: When you accomplish something little or big, take time to celebrate. You earned it!

MAY 11

On this day in 1997: Reigning world chess champion Gary Kasparov loses to IBM computer *Deep Blue*, a first under tournament conditions.

Dive In: Kasparov defeated *Deep Blue* a year earlier, but programing changes sealed his fate in the rematch.

Speak Up: Computers become smarter and smarter over time. Do you think computers should make increasingly more important decisions for people in the future? What problems might arise from computers making decisions for people?

_____

_____

_____

_____

_____

_____

_____

_____

Act Out: Sometimes it's nice to not have to worry about making decisions. However, there's no substitute for knowing what you believe and why you believe it. Become knowledgeable about forces that impact your life so that you can speak up and act out when necessary.

MAY 12

On this day in 2010: Afriqiyah Airways Flight 771 crashes on descent into Tripoli, Libya, killing everyone on board except for one… a 9-year-old boy.

Dive In: The survivor was returning with his family from a Safari when the crash occurred. He suffered two broken legs but no life-threatening injuries.

Speak Up: How would you feel if you were the sole survivor of a disaster—angry, sad, guilty, unworthy, grateful? Do you think the boy survived because he has a special purpose in life, or do you think he was just lucky?

_____

_____

_____

_____

_____

_____

_____

_____

_____

_____

Act Out: Explaining great fortune (or great tragedy) is often an impossible task. Instead, try counting your blessings and making the most of the time you have in this world.

MAY 13

On this day in 1958: Inventor George de Mestral of Switzerland trademarks his "hook and loop" fastener, commonly known as Velcro.

Dive In: Mestral conceived the idea for Velcro after walking through a field with his dog and wondering why burrs stuck to clothing and fur. One look through a microscope told him why and he designed Velcro from his observations. The name Velcro is a combination of two French words: *velour* (velvet) and *crochet* (hook). The rest is history.

Speak Up: How can asking questions about everyday objects help you become smarter about the world around you?

_____

_____

_____

_____

_____

_____

_____

_____

Act Out: Nature, as Mestral discovered, offers a wealth of designs that can make you a lot of money. Be curious and pay close attention to the world around you... you might discover a great invention hiding in plain sight!

MAY 14

On this day in 1948: Israel declares its independence from British control and becomes a sovereign nation for the first time in 2,000 years.

Dive In: Israel as a nation state can be traced back nearly 3,100 years to the rule of King Saul. After the Roman conquest of Israel, the Hebrew people dispersed to various lands around the globe (the *Diaspora*).

Speak Up: Israelites maintained their culture despite migrations to foreign lands. How would you maintain your national, familial, and religious heritage if you migrated to a foreign land? (Hint: what celebrations and customs are most important to you?)

_____

_____

_____

_____

_____

_____

_____

_____

_____

_____

Act Out: Make a list of the occasions your family celebrates. What makes those celebrations special to you?

MAY 15

On this day in 1869: Suffragettes (woman seeking the right to vote) Susan B. Anthony and Elizabeth Cady Stanton form the National Woman Suffrage Association.

Dive In: Susan B. Anthony was arrested and tried for voting in the presidential election of 1872. She was found guilty and fined $100, a sum she refused to pay and never did.

Speak Up: Anthony did not live to see women's suffrage become the law of the land (19th Amendment to US Constitution, 1920) but she laid a firm foundation for its passage. Do you find it hard to play your best (think of a game or sport) when victory seems impossible? What keeps you motivated to continue competing when defeat seems certain?

_____

_____

_____

_____

_____

_____

_____

_____

Act Out: Take your first step to achieve a goal that you're not sure you can accomplish in your lifetime. You'll never know if you can achieve something unless you TRY!

MAY 16

On this day in 1861: Kentucky, USA declares its neutrality in the war between the states (US Civil War).

Dive In: Kentucky's neutrality lasted about four months until both Confederate and Union forces invaded the state. The Legislature passed a resolution calling for the withdrawal of Confederate forces only, officially ending the state's neutral position in the war.

Speak Up: Have you ever got caught up in an argument between friends? Did you try to "stay out of it" or did you take sides? Why did you react the way you did?

_____

_____

_____

_____

_____

_____

_____

_____

_____

_____

Act Out: Staying neutral in arguments, debates, or wars may seem impossible. However, the country of Switzerland has maintained a position of neutrality in military affairs since 1815. Learn more about the Swiss philosophy.

MAY 17

On this day in 1620: The first carousel operates at a fair in Philippapolis, Turkey.

Dive In: The amusement park ride is based on a medieval training exercise for knights. They rode horses in circles and threw balls at each other or practiced jousting at rings suspended above them.

Speak Up: Do you participate in a sport? What techniques does that sport teach you and how might you be able to use them in other areas of life?

_____

_____

_____

_____

_____

_____

_____

_____

_____

_____

Act Out: Games and sports can teach us great life lessons. They prepare us to deal with adversity and work with others to achieve common goals, as well as develop our problem-solving skills. If you aren't involved in sports or games, consider joining a team!

MAY 18

On this day in 2001: 101-year-old golfer Harold Stilson of Boca Raton, FL, USA becomes the oldest person in history to hit a hole-in-one.

Dive In: Stilson's record fell to a 102-year old golfer in 2007. In 2014, a 103-year-old golfer also hit a hole-in-one.

Speak Up: As the saying goes, age is just a number. Which do you think is more important to staying healthy in old age: diet, exercise, or keeping a positive mindset? Explain your answer.

_____

_____

_____

_____

_____

_____

_____

_____

_____

_____

_____

_____

Act Out: If you want to live a long healthy life, find out how others do it. Ask the oldest person you know what they think is the secret to longevity.

MAY 19

On this day in 1883: Buffalo Bill's Wild West show debuts in Omaha, NE, USA.

Dive In: Similar to a circus or carnival, Buffalo Bill's Wild West show incorporated wild animals, tricks, and rodeo stunts, as well as fancy shooting and battle reënactments.

Speak Up: The Wild West show captured the public's romance and nostalgia for a moment in history that was rapidly giving way to modernization. If you could travel back in time to any historical period, where would you go and why?

_____

_____

_____

_____

_____

_____

_____

_____

_____

Act Out: One way to experience history is to act it out. Try your talents in a local drama club or recruit your family and friends to act in a play with you! A great resource for scripts is **https://www.playingwithplays.com/**

MAY 20

On this day in 1932: Amelia Earhart takes off from Harbour Grace, Newfoundland, en route to becoming the first woman to fly non-stop (solo) across the Atlantic.

Dive In: Five years earlier, on the same day, Charles Lindbergh took off from New York in his plane, the Spirit of St. Louis, to become the first person to fly non-stop (solo) across the Atlantic.

Speak Up: Why do you think Earhart chose the anniversary of Lindbergh's flight to begin her own historic journey?

_____

_____

_____

_____

_____

_____

_____

_____

_____

_____

Act Out: In whatever sport, hobby, or career you pursue, learn everything you can about the titans in those fields. They'll serve as inspiration as you aim for ever higher goals.

MAY 21

On this day in 1881: Clara Barton founds the American Red Cross.

Dive In: The Red Cross organization was founded in Switzerland in 1863 by Henry Dunant. Chief among the original goals of the organization was to aid wounded soldiers on the battlefield. The red cross emblem was selected as a reversal of the colors of the Swiss flag in honor of the nation's history of neutrality in military conflicts.

Speak Up: Sometimes a great idea takes off in one country and spreads to another. And another. How do you want to make the world a better place? What organizations share your goals?

_____

_____

_____

_____

_____

_____

_____

_____

Act Out: If you have a big idea to change the world, your success begins by starting small. After finetuning your idea, share it with another person so they can share it with another. And another....

MAY 22

George Kenneth End begins selling canned rattlesnake meat in Florida.

Dive In: Mr. End failed at several business ventures before he tried a bite of rattlesnake. Turns out, rattlesnake tastes like a cross between chicken and quail. By 1940 he was selling 15,000 cans annually. Sadly, in 1943, Mr. End met his end at the fangs of a rattler.

Speak Up: Some food doesn't sound appetizing, but you never know until you taste it. What's the strangest food you ever ate? What's one exotic food that you would like to try?

_____

_____

_____

_____

_____

_____

_____

_____

_____

_____

Act Out: Be daring. Try a food that you have avoided your whole life because it looks gross, smells funny, or just seems plain weird to eat.

MAY 23

On this day in 1430: Joan of Arc, heroine of the Hundred Years' War, is captured in battle and sold to the English.

Dive In: The English were convinced that Joan of Arc was possessed by the Devil, despite her impeccable character and strict adherence to God. She was charged with Heresy, but when that failed to garner a sentence of death, she was charged with cross-dressing. For this crime, she was burned at the stake at the age of 19.

Speak Up: As a young peasant girl, Joan received visions from Angels of God to drive out the English from France. With no military experience, she acted on these visions and turned the tide of the war. Have you ever been too afraid to do something because you didn't know how to do it? What was it?

_____

_____

_____

_____

_____

_____

_____

Act Out: Beginning is often that hardest part of succeeding. Don't worry if you don't know what you're doing—you'll learn all you need to know by taking action.

MAY 24

On this day in 1964: Stampede during soccer match in Lima, Peru kills 328.

Dive In: After the referee waved-off a tying goal by the home team in the late minutes of the match, fans stormed the field. Police fired tear gas to disperse the crowd and panic ensued.

Speak Up: What's the largest crowd you've ever been in and what was the occasion? Do you like being in large crowds, or do you prefer hanging out with a small group of people? Why?

_____

_____

_____

_____

_____

_____

_____

_____

_____

_____

Act Out: A "herd mentality" means following what everyone else is doing. This can be dangerous whether you're in the midst of a crowd or following at a distance. Always think about *what* you're doing and *why* you're doing it!

MAY 25

On this day in 1935: Track and field athlete Jesse Owens sets three world records and equals a fourth in a span of 45 minutes.

Dive In: Jesse Owens continued his winning ways the next year at the Berlin Summer Olympics, winning 4 gold medals (three individual and one team relay.)

Speak Up: Have you ever had a day where everything seemed to go your way? Have you ever had a day where nothing seemed to go your way? What do you think is the biggest difference between success and failure?

_____

_____

_____

_____

_____

_____

_____

_____

_____

Act Out: Pass it on. Owens attributed his athletic success to the encouragement of his junior high school coach. Become a mentor to someone younger than you. Help them achieve their dreams.

MAY 26

On this day in 2002: NASA's Mars Odyssey orbiter detects an abundance of water ice below the planet's surface; enough water, perhaps, to fill Lake Michigan twice.

Dive In: Martian water will be crucial for a successful manned mission to Mars. Key to the discovery is that the water ice lies less than a meter below the surface, meaning astronauts won't need heavy equipment to get to it—they can dig it up with shovels.

Speak Up: A manned mission to Mars might be a one-way trip, unless scientists figure out how to make rocket fuel from material on Mars. Would you travel to Mars if you knew you could never return to Earth? Explain your answer.

_____

_____

_____

_____

_____

_____

_____

_____

_____

_____

Act Out: List three reason why building a city on Mars would be beneficial to mankind.

MAY 27

On this day in 1995: Actor Christopher Reeve, best known for playing Superman in the Hollywood action movie franchise, is paralyzed from the neck down after falling from his horse.

Dive In: Though paralyzed, Reeve returned to acting and directing following his injury and became a prominent advocate for spinal cord injury research.

Speak Up: Reeve demonstrated that while injuries may change the course of someone's life, the injury may also serve as a platform to accomplish important work. Have you ever suffered an injury or defeat that opened a door to other opportunities?

_____

_____

_____

_____

_____

_____

_____

_____

_____

Act Out: Have a fallback plan. You may not be able to do what you love most forever.

MAY 28

On this day in 1901: First laws against white phosphorus in friction matches go into effect.

Dive In: White phosphorus matches made starting fires a snap for consumers. For workers in match factories, however, the chemical caused terrible illness, including "phossy jaw", an ailment marked by tooth loss and rot of the lower jaw.

Speak Up: "Phossy jaw" usually surfaced in workers exposed to white phosphorus for five years or longer. Have you ever done something that seemed harmless in the moment but caused you pain later? What lesson did you learn from it?

_____

_____

_____

_____

_____

_____

_____

_____

_____

Act Out: Just because something doesn't harm you this minute, or this day, or this month doesn't mean it isn't causing long term damage to your health. Take good care of your body by watching what you eat, drink, breathe, and apply to your skin.

MAY 29

On this day in 1942: Bing Crosby records the song *White Christmas* (written by Irving Berlin) which goes on to sell more than 50 million copies.

Dive In: Prior to Bing Crosby's song, marketers had not targeted Christmastime with themes of longing for home and days gone by. All that changed with Crosby's performance.

Speak Up: Do some holidays or seasons make you long for your family or the past? What holiday/season is it? Why do you think it dredges up those emotions in you?

_____

_____

_____

_____

_____

_____

_____

_____

_____

Act Out: Ah, the holidays! They serve as a break from our mundane or hectic schedules and leave us with memories that last a lifetime. We often look back on them as much as we look forward to them. Cherish them!

MAY 30

On this day in 1868: Decoration Day (later renamed Memorial Day) is first observed in portions of the US.

Dive In: Following the US Civil War, families of fallen soldiers wished to honor their memory by decorating homes and businesses with flags. The tradition took root.

Speak Up: Remembering the sacrifices of our ancestors is a time worn tradition. What are three facts or stories your parents have shared with you about your deceased ancestors?

_____

_____

_____

_____

_____

_____

_____

_____

_____

_____

_____

_____

Act Out: Part of remembering the past is recording events in the present. If you haven't already done so, use the *Outro* pages of this book to write down significant family events. *Your* ancestors will thank you for the insights!

MAY 31

On this day in 1279 BC: Ramesses II becomes Pharaoh of Egypt.

Dive In: Recognized as the greatest ruler of ancient Egypt, Ramesses II ruled for 66 years and dedicated his reign to constructing cities, monuments, and temples.

Speak Up: Ramesses built a legacy that has survived 3,300 years! What legacy do you plan to leave behind for your family, friends, and the world? What can you do today to establish your legacy?

_____

_____

_____

_____

_____

_____

_____

_____

_____

_____

Act Out: First things first. If you haven't yet decided what you want to be remembered for, there's no time like the present to figure it out. Start with your goal, then add up the steps you need to take to make it happen.

MAY
OUTRO

Time Capsule: _____
_____
_____
_____

I chased my dreams by: _____
_____
_____
_____

I made the world a better place by: _____
_____
_____
_____

I'm looking forward to: _____
_____
_____
_____

Next play: _____
_____

JUNE
INTRO

*"We must believe that we are gifted for something,
and that this thing, at whatever cost,
must be attained."*

\- Marie Curie

JUNE 1

On this day in 1908: John "Colonial Jack" Krohn, dressed in colonial-style clothing and pushing a wheelbarrow, begins his 9,042 mile walk around the US border.

Dive In: Krohn's journey began as a wager with friends that he could not accomplish the walk in less than 400 days. He did it in 357. The wheelbarrow was a requirement so that he could not hitch rides. Krohn's friends also required him to get 635 cancellation stamps from post offices along his route.

Speak Up: Dedicating almost a year of your life to any cause is quite an investment. What might you learn about yourself and your country by completing such a walk?

_____

_____

_____

_____

_____

_____

_____

_____

_____

_____

Act Out: Take a walk around your neighborhood or downtown. Visit historical sites in your city to learn more about your city's history.

JUNE 2

On this day in 1975: First June snowfall ever recorded in London.

Dive In: When June rolls around, we generally look forward to sunshine and beaches. But a worldwide cooling trend that began in 1945 led some scientists to worry that shortened growing seasons would lead to food shortages.

Speak Up: What negative effects would we experience if the world cooled? How about if it warmed?

_____

_____

_____

_____

_____

_____

_____

_____

_____

_____

_____

_____

Act Out: A record low temperature yesterday or a record high temperature tomorrow doesn't mean much. We must look at long term trends, that is, the big picture. Drawing conclusions with more information improves your results.

JUNE 3

On this day in 1989: The Tiananmen Square Massacre begins as Chinese soldiers open fire on pro-democracy activists.

Dive In: At the height of the protests, nearly a million citizens descended on Tiananmen Square. In response, the communist Chinese government mobilized 300,000 troops to Beijing. An estimated 2,600 people died in the crackdown.

Speak Up: Democratic nations have largely turned a blind eye to human rights abuses in China, placing greater value on cheap products from the country than human rights for the Chinese citizens who make them. Do you think we set a good example for freedom when we enrich ourselves through the oppression of others? Why or why not?

_____

_____

_____

_____

_____

_____

_____

_____

Act Out: Look at a product label in your home (clothes, toys, electronics, etc.) to find out where it was made. Learn three facts about that country.

JUNE 4

On this day in 1984: Scientists clone DNA from an extinct animal (quagga) for the first time.

Dive In: Quagga, a subspecies of zebra, went extinct in the 19th century.

Speak Up: The movie series *Jurassic Park* explored the issue of cloning extinct animals. What extinct animal would you like to see cloned? Would you rather visit a zoo filled with extant animals or clones from extinct animals? Why?

_____

_____

_____

_____

_____

_____

_____

_____

_____

_____

_____

_____

Act Out: Is cloning extinct animals a good idea? (List two reasons why it might be good and two reasons why it might be bad.)

JUNE 5

On this day in 1851: Harriet Beecher Stowe's anti-slavery novel *Uncle Tom's Cabin* first published in serial form in the *National Era*.

Dive In: Published the next year in book form, *Uncle Tom's Cabin* went on to become the best-selling novel of the 19th century. Many credit Stowe's fiction with changing public opinion about the institution of slavery.

Speak Up: Have you ever read a book that opened your eyes to something terribly unfair in the world? What book was it?

_____

_____

_____

_____

_____

_____

_____

_____

_____

_____

Act Out: We understand the struggles of people better when we hear their life stories. This is true for historical and fictional characters. Read a biography about someone who struggled for change or faced lifelong oppression.

JUNE 6

On this day in 1816: Ten inches of snow falls in New England. Called the "year without a summer" thereafter, many crops fail, and famine follows.

Dive In: The severe plunge of summer temperatures around the world can be traced to the April 1815 eruption of Mount Tambora in Indonesia.

Speak Up: We don't often think of events half way around the world as affecting our lives, but sometimes they do. Would your family have enough food on hand to sustain you if the "year without summer" repeated itself?

_____

_____

_____

_____

_____

_____

_____

_____

_____

_____

Act Out: Be prepared. 1816 is a long time ago! But that doesn't mean long ago events can't repeat in our own day and age. Pay careful attention to events around the world.

JUNE 7

On this day in 1665: Samuel Pepys records in his diary events of the Great Plague in London: houses are marked with red crosses to alert the community that someone inside is infected and must remain quarantined for 40 days until healthy or dead.

Dive In: In the years of 2020-2021, many countries faced lockdowns due to coronavirus. Gone were the red crosses on doors, replaced by "contract tracing" utilizing Internet apps.

Speak Up: Sometimes individual liberties butt up against community welfare. Which do you think is more important: living your life as you choose, or keeping the community safe? Explain your answer.

_____

_____

_____

_____

_____

_____

_____

_____

_____

_____

Act Out: Live in balance. Take care of yourself and your family. You cannot help others when you are not well.

JUNE 8

On this day in 1789: James Madison proposes a Bill of Rights to the US Constitution.

Dive In: Many argued that Madison's Bill of Rights was unnecessary because the US Constitution only granted specific rights to the federal government; therefore, all unspecified rights were retained by the individual States and the people.

Speak Up: Madison was a man who had been fooled in the past and didn't want to get fooled again. Have you ever agreed to a bargain with someone, only to feel cheated after the fact? What was it and how could you have protected yourself better?

_____

_____

_____

_____

_____

_____

_____

_____

Act Out: Get that in writing. When entering into a contract with someone else, make sure you clarify everything you are agreeing to, in writing, before signing your name to it. That way, you both know what's expected of the agreement.

JUNE 9

On this day in 1549: The Church of England adopts the *Book of Common Prayer.*

Dive In: What do you say when someone falls ill, when someone dies, when someone marries, or a child is born? *The Book of Common Prayer* answers these questions and more, drawing from centuries of religious practice.

Speak Up: The *Book of Common Prayer* has undergone numerous refinements over the years, but more or less held true to the 1662 edition. Do you think a book that guides your words in extraordinary times is a good thing, or would you rather just speak what's in your heart? Explain your answer.

_____

_____

_____

_____

_____

_____

_____

_____

_____

Act Out: Sometimes life comes at us fast. Do you struggle to find appropriate words in unexpected events? *The Book of Common Prayer* may help clarify your thoughts.

JUNE 10

False Dimitry I is crowned Tsar of Russia.

Dive In: Dimitry, son of Ivan the Terrible, was assassinated in 1591. False Dimitry, however, adopted his identity and claimed the assassination attempt had failed. He fooled many with his lie, and convinced others to go along with the charade for political reasons, including the real Dimitry's own mother.

Speak Up: False Dimitry would have stood no chance of becoming Tsar apart from his lie, despite his education and ability to build alliances with influential people. What benefits can a good family name bring to a person that education and accomplishments cannot?

_____

_____

_____

_____

_____

_____

_____

_____

Act Out: People tend to trust members of families that have good reputations. Aim to build a respected name for yourself and make your family proud.

JUNE 11

On this day in 1184 BC: The city of Troy is invaded and burned by the Greeks, ending the 10-year Trojan War.

Dive In: In Greek mythology, the Greeks gave the city of Troy a large wooden horse, which they wheeled inside the city walls. That night, Greek soldiers climbed out of the horse and conquered the Trojans.

Speak Up: Enemies usually don't give gifts to each other—that should have been the Trojans first clue that all was not right! Would you be suspicious if someone you didn't know offered you a gift? Would you accept it, or politely decline?

_____

_____

_____

_____

_____

_____

_____

_____

_____

_____

Act Out: Scams have existed throughout history. Be leery of strangers offering you unsolicited gifts, not only in person, but by e-mail or other Internet sites.

JUNE 12

On this day in 1942: 13-year-old Anne Frank receives a diary for her birthday.

Dive In: Anne Frank's diary is arguably the most famous diary in history. Her first-hand account of Jewish life under Nazi occupation has enlightened and inspired millions of readers.

Speak Up: Do you think you should only write about "important" events in a diary? How might "ordinary" events happening to you today become important to you in the future?

_____
_____
_____
_____
_____
_____
_____
_____
_____
_____

Act Out: You might be tempted to think that nothing remarkable happened to you yesterday or today, but we often don't recognize important events as they are happening to us. Keep writing your story!

JUNE 13

On this day in 1920: The US Post Office issues a directive that children may not be sent by parcel post.

Dive In: Strange as it sounds, several instances of parents shipping young children through the mail with postage stamps stuck to their clothes occurred before this directive was issued.

Speak Up: Would you feel lonely/scared to travel alone, or would you see it as a great adventure? Where in the world would you go if allowed to travel by yourself?

_____

_____

_____

_____

_____

_____

_____

_____

_____

_____

_____

Act Out: A good book is sort of like taking a trip alone. Of course, the characters in the story become our traveling companions. Find a book to read about the destination you mentioned in the *Speak Up* section above.

JUNE 14

Captain Bligh and 17 loyalists, having survived a mutiny and 47 days at sea in a launch, arrive in Timor.

Dive In: The mutiny on the HMS *Bounty* occurred after the botanical mission left Tahiti for England. The mutineers returned to Tahiti where many of them were apprehended the following year by the HMS *Pandora*. Several mutineers escaped, however, sailing the *Bounty* to Pitcairn Island, where they sank the ship and lived out their days.

Speak Up: The idea of living on a tropical island appeals to lots of people. If you moved to a tropical island with no modern technology, what would you miss most? How would you spend your leisure time when you weren't catching fish or foraging for roots, fruits, and vegetables?

_____

_____

_____

_____

_____

_____

_____

Act Out: Sometimes we find ourselves in situations we wish we could escape. Before you agree to anything, think carefully about the consequences.

JUNE 15

On this day in 1667: Dr. Jean-Batiste Denys, a French physician, performs the first known human blood transfusion on a 15-year-old boy.

Dive In: Dr. Denys did not transfuse human blood to the boy; rather, he used sheep blood. Remarkably, the boy survived.

Speak Up: If you suffered from a grave illness, would you agree to an untested medical treatment? Why or why not?

_____

_____

_____

_____

_____

_____

_____

_____

_____

_____

_____

Act Out: Today, blood transfusions are common and the need for blood donors high. When you're old enough, consider becoming a blood donor (you usually get free cookies or donuts after donating)!

JUNE 16

On this day in 1784: The Netherlands forbids wearing orange clothing of any kind.

Dive In: Why would a country forbid citizens from wearing a certain color of clothing? At the time, orange was associated with the magistrates, who were seen as wielding too much influence over political affairs. When commoners began wearing orange bows and ribbons in support of the magistrates, enough was enough!

Speak Up: Do you have a favorite color? What is it and why do you like it the best? Are there any colors you wouldn't wear no matter what? Why?

_____

_____

_____

_____

_____

_____

_____

_____

_____

_____

Act Out: Today, orange is the symbolic color of the Netherlands, worn at national festivals and sporting events. Wear your favorite color today to celebrate *you*!

JUNE 17

On this day in 1631: Mumtaz Mahal, bride of Mughal emperor Shah Jahan, dies giving birth to their 14th child. The emperor spends the next 22 years constructing her majestic resting place—the Taj Mahal.

Dive In: As far as acts of love and devotion go, few in history compare to Shah Jahan's. The complex of gateway, gardens, mosque, and mausoleum covers 42 acres of land. When Shah Jahan died in 1658, he was entombed beside his wife in the lower level of the mausoleum.

Speak Up: If money were no object (the Taj Mahal would cost about billion dollars to build today), how would you memorialize the love of your life? Or, would you choose a simpler, less ostentatious memorial? Why?

_____

_____

_____

_____

_____

_____

_____

_____

Act Out: Love is a verb. Don't just tell those you care about how much they mean to you. Show them in your own way.

JUNE 18

On this day in 1980: Indian mathematician Shakuntala Devi correctly multiplies two random 13-digit numbers in 28 seconds... in her head!

Dive In: No calculator. No computer. No problem. Devi had her brains. By correctly multiplying 7,686,369,774,870 x 2,465,099,745,779 she set a world record.

Speak Up: Setting yourself up for failure is no way to succeed. How many times have you said something was impossible before you even tried? Give an example.

_____

_____

_____

_____

_____

_____

_____

_____

_____

_____

_____

_____

Act Out: Many great achievements and discoveries were made when people approached an "impossible" problem with the idea that a solution existed... it just needed to be found. If you want to achieve the "impossible", keep that mindset!

JUNE 19

On this day in 1865: Union General Gordon Granger declares an end to slavery in Texas. The day is commonly celebrated as an end to US slavery, known as Juneteenth.

Dive In: Although Juneteenth is celebrated as the end of US slavery, slavery was still practiced in Delaware and Kentucky until the ratification of the 13th amendment (abolition of slavery) on December 6, 1865.

Speak Up: Many groups argue that Juneteenth is such an important date in American history that it ought to be a national holiday. Do you think it should be a national holiday? Why or why not?

_____

_____

_____

_____

_____

_____

_____

_____

_____

Act Out: The US has 10 national holidays and opponents of new holidays argue this is enough. Should a great country be limited to only 10 important events? Celebrate *all* important events—the more the better!

JUNE 20

English aviator Sheila Scott completes the first solo airplane flight by a woman around the world.

Dive In: Scott's flight began and ended at London Heathrow spanning over 31,000 miles and lasting 34 days (189 hours of flight time.)

Speak Up: Few of us can say we did something that nobody before us did. What world record would you be the proudest to hold? Do you believe you can achieve your goal?

_____

_____

_____

_____

_____

_____

_____

_____

_____

_____

_____

_____

_____

Act Out: Doing adventurous things on your own requires guts. Flying around the world would be one of them. Set a goal for yourself that requires you to rely on nobody but you.

JUNE 21

On this day in 1954: Runner John Landy becomes the second person to run a mile in under four minutes (3:58:00).

Dive In: Roger Bannister had become the first human in history to run a sub-four-minute mile only 46 days earlier. That summer, the two runners faced off in what became known as the "Miracle Mile." Bannister bested Landy on his way to setting a new world record in a race notable for featuring two runners, for the first time, who slapped a mile under foot in less than four minutes.

Speak Up: Before Bannister and Landy ran their record times, scientists claimed it was impossible for humans to run so fast; in fact, they said it might kill anyone attempting to do so. Today, high school kids run sub-four-minute miles. Why can many people do today what nobody in all of history could do until 1954?

_____

_____

_____

_____

_____

Act Out: Conceive. Believe. Achieve. Bannister and Landy set goals, believed they could accomplish them, and pushed themselves hard enough to achieve them. You are no less able than they to achieve your dreams. Just do it!

JUNE 22

On this day in 1633: The Catholic Church, under Pope Urban VIII, convicts astronomer Galileo Galilei of heresy regarding his belief that the Earth orbits the Sun, not the other way around.

Dive In: The commonly held belief at the time, that the Earth was the center of the universe, and everything (including the Sun) revolved around it, was wrong. The Catholic Church did not admit its error until 1992!

Speak Up: Hey, it's hard to be wrong. We've all been there. But holding to a false belief is a bad idea. How could the Catholic Church have responded to Galileo's discoveries in a better way? (They sentenced him to house arrest for the rest of this life.)

_____

_____

_____

_____

_____

_____

_____

_____

_____

_____

Act Out: Own up to your mistakes. The sooner the better!

JUNE 23

On this day in 1926: The College Board administers the first SAT test in America.

Dive In: College admissions offices state that SAT scores are not the predominant factor in admissions. However, they help to measure the aptitude of students seeking admission to the college, along with high school grades over time and extracurricular activities.

Speak Up: Why is it important to do your best on tests? Have you ever *not* performed your best because you didn't think it would matter?

_____

_____

_____

_____

_____

_____

_____

_____

Act Out: Marilyn McGrath, onetime director of undergraduate admissions at Harvard College, put it this way: "You have to have done well in all the things you put your mind to do" to get admitted to Harvard. Don't slack off. Do your absolute best at everything!

JUNE 24

On this day in 1947: Private pilot Kenneth Arnold sights a string of nine unidentified flying objects (UFOs) over Mount Rainier (WA, USA).

Dive In: Based on Arnold's description of the crafts, the media quickly named these objects "Flying Saucers."

Speak Up: An *unidentified flying object* simply means that something observed in flight cannot be identified by known or typical observations. Does that mean it is extraterrestrial in origin? What do you think?

_____

_____

_____

_____

_____

_____

_____

_____

_____

_____

_____

_____

Act Out: Be sure of your observations and gather all the facts. We may see something strange and jump to fantastic conclusions, only to learn later it has a mundane explanation.

JUNE 25

On this day in 1876: The Battle of Little Big Horn ends when Sioux and Cheyenne warriors crush the US 7th Cavalry Regiment commanded by Lt. Col. George Custer.

Dive In: Custer's Last Stand, as the battle came to be known, resulted from Custer misjudging the size of the enemy battle force. He understood the force to be roughly equal to his own when in fact it outnumbered the 7th Cavalry Regiment 2-3 times.

Speak Up: Have you ever felt unprepared and overwhelmed? Was it because you didn't take your preparation seriously, or because you didn't understand what was required of you?

_____

_____

_____

_____

_____

_____

_____

_____

Act Out: Count the cost before beginning anything. Know what it will take to complete what you set out to do. If you are not prepared to meet the demands of your goal, you are better off delaying the goal or not pursuing it at all.

JUNE 26

On this day in 1945: 50 nations sign the Charter of the United Nations in San Francisco, CA, USA.

Dive In: The Allied powers of WWII understood the need to establish a postwar organization to promote and maintain peace and security. The war wrought terrible destruction that no member countries wished to see repeated.

Speak Up: WWI was called the "war to end all wars," and yet less than 20 years later WWII began. Have you ever repeated a mistake that you swore you would never make again? What got you into that mess?

_____

_____

_____

_____

_____

_____

_____

_____

_____

_____

Act Out: Our poor decisions today can prepare us to make better decisions tomorrow. Learn from your mistakes and lapses in judgment.

JUNE 27

On this day in 1915: The hottest temperature ever recorded in the state of Alaska (Fort Yukon, AK, USA) – 100° F.

Dive In: We often think of Alaska as an icebox of glaciers and polar bears, but it can get hot up there.

Speak Up: Describe the hottest day you can remember. How do you like to cool off when outdoor temperatures rise? Sprinklers, swimming pools, water balloon fights, maybe a popsicle or two?

_____

_____

_____

_____

_____

_____

_____

_____

_____

_____

_____

Act Out: Even when it's blazing hot outside, you can make the most of a bad situation. Find some shade, drink some lemonade, or better yet, find an air-conditioned retreat to wait out the heat!

JUNE 28

On this day in 1820: Colonel Robert Gibbon dispels an American myth that the tomato is poisonous by eating one publicly on the steps of a New Jersey courthouse.

Dive In: Tomatoes, also known as the "wolf peach," had been eaten for years in Europe and South America, but due to bad information the fruit was blacklisted from the grocery lists of many Americans.

Speak Up: How do we know if a food is poisonous or not? Usually, someone must eat the substance and survive. Why would someone risk eating a plant that could kill them?

_____

_____

_____

_____

_____

_____

_____

_____

_____

_____

_____

Act Out: Just because something tastes pleasant doesn't mean it is okay to eat (or drink). Never ingest something without knowing the effects it may have on your health!

JUNE 29

On this day in 1940: In the Batman Comics, mobsters kill a family circus highwire team known as the "Flying Graysons," orphaning their son, Dick (Robin).

Dive In: Every Batman has his Robin. Every Lone Ranger has his Tanto. Sidekicks are popular not just in comics, but in everyday life.

Speak Up: Life without a sidekick can be pretty bland. Who is your best friend? What makes your friendship more special than any other?

_____

_____

_____

_____

_____

_____

_____

_____

_____

_____

_____

Act Out: As the Bible puts it, "Two are better than one... for if they fall, one will lift up his fellow." Cherish your friendships. They enrich life like nothing else!

JUNE 30

On this day in 1908: A massive explosion, thought to be caused by a giant comet, levels an estimated 80 million trees near the Tunguska River in Russia (Tunguska Event).

Dive In: Thankfully, whatever hit the Earth that day did so in a sparsely populated area. Had the "comet" exploded above a major city, the city may have been wiped out!

Speak Up: Sometimes we take life for granted. Do you ever worry that something unexpected, like an asteroid or comet, will wreck everything? What about less devastating impacts on your life, like bad grades or mean social media posts?

_____

_____

_____

_____

_____

_____

_____

_____

_____

Act Out: Keep life in perspective. Some events, like the death of a friend or relative, weigh heavy on our hearts. Others, like the cruelty or thoughtlessness of others, affect us only as much as we allow them to. Be strong and never let the words or actions of others flatten you.

JUNE
OUTRO

Time Capsule: _____
_____
_____
_____

I chased my dreams by: _____
_____
_____
_____

I made the world a better place by: _____
_____
_____
_____

I'm looking forward to: _____
_____
_____
_____

Next play: _____
_____

6-month *Goals*

3-year *Goals*

_____

_____

_____

_____

_____

_____

_____

_____

_____

_____

_____

_____

_____

_____

_____

_____

_____

_____

_____

_____

_____

_____

_____

_____

_____

_____

_____

_____

_____

_____

Lifetime *Goals*

ABOUT THE AUTHOR

J.C. Dublin grew up in New England, West Germany, and Northern Virginia; and is a graduate of The University of Arizona. He lives in the Pacific Northwest with his wife and four children.

Made in the USA
Monee, IL
31 May 2021